THE
PAINTED
BEDROOM
AND BATHROOM

Bedroom and bathrooms are 'retreat' spaces – a step back from the harder working living areas such as kitchens and living rooms. For this reason such space offers particular opportunities for personal and imaginative expression – and what better approach than painted decoration?

The Painted Bedroom and Bathroom is a practical and inspirational guide to atmospheric painted room treatments, complete with a substantial section of specially photographed and colourful paint finishes, motifs and effects, carefully prepared for the non-professional. The book includes a wide range of styles, and gives expert hints and tips on detailing and accessorizing for maximum effect. Clearly written and presented, this book is a lively and original source of ideas and practical guidance which will appeal to every creative home decorator.

Susan Berry has written a number of books on interiors, decorating and garden design. She is the author of *Decorating Entrances, Stairways and Landings.*

THE
PAINTED
BEDROOM
AND BATHROOM

Ideas and inspirations for the creative home decorator

SUSAN BERRY

CASSELL

A CASSELL BOOK

This edition 1995 by
Cassell
Wellington House
125 Strand
London WC2R 0BB

Distributed in the United States by Sterling Publishing Co. Inc.
387 Park Avenue South, New York, NY 10016–8810

Distributed in Australia by Capricorn Link (Australia) Pty Ltd
2/13 Carrington Road, Castle Hill, NSW 2154

British Library Cataloguing-in-Publication Data
A catalogue record for this book is available from the
British Library

ISBN 0–304–34732–9

Designed by Richard Carr

Typeset by RGM, The Mews, Birkdale Village, Southport, England

Printed and bound in Great Britain by The Bath Press

CONTENTS

INSPIRATION FOR DECORATION

THIS PART of the book covers the basic elements of decorating with paint, including an understanding of style, colour and period. Bedrooms and bathrooms are, however, only one small part of a flat or house, and any scheme for these rooms does need to be considered as part of the overall decoration.

There is a growing trend, today, for more unified decorating schemes, and a move away from each different part of the house being treated as a separate entity, so try to think of ways to link the bedroom and bathroom decoration with that of the rest of the house, either with colour, pattern or furnishing style.

INTRODUCTION

This Gustavian-style bedroom in soft blues and yellows has made good use of a range of paint effects, and the colours have been combined with great artistry. The bed has been colour-washed and gilded, while the central panel of the end board has been painted freehand. The walls have been colour-washed in pale yellow, with an acid yellow border to define them, and a panel behind the bedside table has been colour-washed and antiqued around a papered motif.

PAINT IS about the cheapest form of decoration and, at its simplest, the easiest that the amateur home decorator can opt for. If you want to give an instant facelift to any room in the house, then paint it. The choice of colour determines the mood, as do the texture and the way the surface reflects or absorbs light. You are not just limited to the fixtures – the walls, ceilings, floors, doors and windows; you can paint almost any element in the room you choose – furniture, lampshades, mirror and picture frames, and even fabrics.

In every era, there is a marked preference for a particular style. This varies from country to country, although there is now a growing element of 'international' taste, influenced by ideas culled from articles in magazines on design and decoration, syndicated worldwide. From this pantheon of styles, colours and designs, you have to choose what will suit you, your lifestyle and your practical requirements.

It is a good idea to work out *why* certain colours, styles and schemes appeal to you. For most of us, it is simply not possible to transform a room every time a particular colour or style goes in or out of fashion. It pays, therefore, not to follow fashion too slavishly. Look elsewhere than in magazines for inspiration and try to determine which colours, shapes and textures you respond to most positively. Many of these responses are based on childhood memories – pleasant or otherwise – and although this is no bad thing, it is also a good plan to expand your ideas. To choose colours simply because your mother or grandmother did is not necessarily going to make you particularly happy. Nor, frankly, is choosing the diametric opposite! Try to work out whether you respond best to cool or warm surfaces, rough or shiny textures, clutter or space. For most of us, some of these responses change according to our circumstances. The kind of colour and style choice that would suit a city pied-à-terre would be very different from that chosen for a country house.

However, you are not obliged to opt for slick, modern, pared-down designs simply because you do live in a city. Maybe you are temporarily stuck in an urban environment, but prefer the countryside. One way of evoking the latter is to recreate the style, colours and shapes in your town home.

We associate colours with familiar things, so one of the easiest ways of giving a room a 'town' feel or a 'country' feel is to use colour to do so. Advertising agencies recognize exactly how people associate colours with familiar situations and objects and use this mercilessly to sell their products. It is no accident that medical products are frequently packaged in pale blue containers – blue is deemed to be cool, hygienic, passive and unthreatening, evoking images of water, ice, cleanliness, while a new brand of wholemeal biscuits will be wrapped in a brown and gold package – images of sun, harvest, the good earth, wholesomeness. There is a whole range of images associated with colours and although there are no hard and fast rules, there is definitely a strong association in our minds for many of them. A strong black and white colour scheme, with touches of red, gives the impression of slickness, sophistication and smartness. Soft, pale pastel colours give the impression of femininity, charm and softness.

You can, rather successfully, swing a few surprises, mixing unusual colours together or using them in untypical ways to create visual interest and excitement, but there is a danger that the plan may misfire, and simply look a mess. In order to play with colour, you need to know the likely effects, and to understand how tone and saturation (see page 13) affect your choices.

You should consider the architectural features of any room, and its contents, before you decide on a particular scheme for the decoration. Try to make the most of any obvious features – fireplaces, windows, cornices and so forth, perhaps using a particular colour to unite certain aspects of the architecture. If the room is unremittingly dull, with no interesting features, then consider adding them. For example, a chair rail or imitation cornice is not difficult, or expensive, to put up and can help greatly to give the room a more distinctive look.

This wood-panelled bedroom has a deceptively simple colour scheme. Painted in pale yellow, it has a higher than normal chair rail picked out in blue, which has also been used to surround the architrave to the door, while the same blue picks out a stencilled border at cornice height. The limed wood floor and the simple furniture give the room an attractively artless, country feel.

Although you may well want to create an appropriate 'period' look for your house, I find it deeply unimaginative to decorate a Victorian terraced house, for example, in an entirely Victorian style. Frankly, I would rather visit a museum. Copying any specific period style seems unnecessarily arch, especially if carried to extremes. A far better solution is to do what all good designers have done over the centuries: appropriate a few elements that work for you and incorporate them with other ideas, thereby giving your home a strongly personal flavour. It is, however, worth noting any particular period features and borrowing some, if not all, of the emblems of that style – for example, the Georgian colour palette – pastel greens, blues and pinks – or Victorian polychromy – a vibrant mixture of dark, glowing colours.

COLOUR

THE MOST important element to consider is colour. The effect that colour has on mood is marked, and well-documented by psychologists. Its importance is now taken into account when planning colour schemes for public buildings to create appropriate responses. Blue, for example, is supposed to induce a feeling of reflection and tranquillity, while yellow is supposed to make you feel warmer and happier.

Such is the power of colour that it can even affect other senses: for example, a red-painted room is generally perceived as actually feeling warmer than a blue-painted one, which has the same temperature. Colour also affects our assessment of size and shape, and weight and distance. A blue object will appear smaller and further away than a red one of the same size at the same distance will seem.

Another important consideration when planning a colour scheme is to make sure that the various elements work well together. It is often surprising to find that a colour scheme which you dreamed up on paper does not

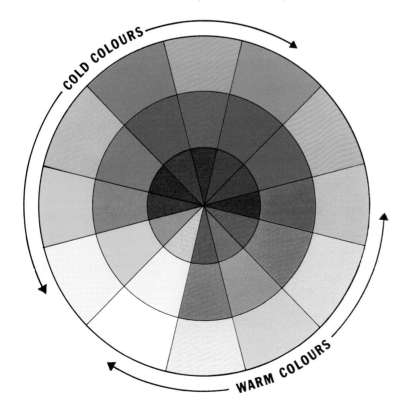

COLD COLOURS

WARM COLOURS

The colour wheel is made up of the three primary colours – red, yellow and blue – and the colours that link these together. The colours that are opposite each other on the wheel contrast (what are known as complementary colours) while those next to each other blend.

translate well to a larger area. This is probably because you did not grasp that the proportion of one colour to another affects the way it is perceived. If you imagine a scheme for a dado, chair rail, wall and picture rail using, say, a pale sage green, a deeper sage green, and a rusty Indian red, it would look completely different if you picked out the dado in the dark green, the chair rail and picture rail in the rusty red and the upper part of the walls in the paler green than it would if you picked out the dado in pale green, the upper part of the wall in the rusty red and the chair rail and picture rail in the darker green.

A common mistake in planning colour schemes for interior decoration is to be too precise in the choice of colours, particularly when you are dealing with large areas, such as walls. The tone becomes as important as the colour, and so does the saturation (see box) in getting the colour relationship right.

One of the more recent innovations in painting and decoration is to use several tones of the same colour for a room. This is a particularly useful way to lend interest to a room without making it look bitty. Dividing up large areas of wall surface with different colours will make them look smaller, and these colour divisions can be used for specific purposes to change the room's proportions. A room with a very high ceiling could be much improved by dividing up the wall area with a dado and picture rail, and painting the areas in different shades of the same colour.

HOW COLOURS WORK

As every schoolchild knows, there are three primary colours: yellow, red and blue. Every other colour is a mixture of these with the addition possibly of white or black. A colour which has no white or black added to it is called highly saturated – its purity or intensity is greatest. When white is added, the colour lightens in tone but loses saturation. When black is added, it darkens in tone and also loses saturation.

When planning a colour scheme, take notice of the tone and saturation of the colours you choose. They are as important in the success of the end result as compatibility of colour contrasts. If one colour – a soft, brownish pink, for example – is subtly greyed, it may simply look dingy against a colour which is particularly pure in tone – say, a bright blue – but it would look wonderful combined with a colour with a similar tonal value – misty taupe or cloudy violet, for example.

Opposite   Strong colours can be made to work well if the theme is kept simple. Here, the roughly plastered walls have been colour-washed a deep cobalt blue over a white ground (you could achieve the same effect on smooth plaster using a technique known as frottage, described on page 70). The same blue in a matt finish paint has been used to pick out the window frame and slatted shutters. Crisp white bedlinen on the white iron-frame bed makes a good contrast with it.

LIGHT

Light plays a major part in choosing any colour scheme, and like colour, it affects our mood greatly. Some people seem to be particularly sensitive to lack of light, and cannot bear dark rooms, or dark colours. Others enjoy the womb-like cosiness of dark rooms, and feel more comfortable in them. Whichever

Spare bedrooms are increasingly being turned into bathrooms. Here, a wonderful old roll-top bath, its sides painted with an imitation wood finish in horizontal panels, is offset by the soft terracotta walls, painted in a quasi-dragged effect in two tones, to create subtle stripes.

you respond to, it is important to remember that you will certainly have strong feelings about it. Don't be influenced, again, by what is fashionable but follow your gut-instinct.

If you like light colours, but dislike the feeling of coldness that pure white gives, it pays to tint the white slightly to remove the blueness, using a warm-toned colour like yellow or apricot, and to find other ways of softening the impact, using rougher matt textures and soft fabrics.

INSPIRATION FOR COLOUR SCHEMES

W HEN IT comes to deciding on a colour scheme for a room, it is often helpful to have a close look at some of the contents: furniture, fabrics or ceramics. Try to put aside any prejudices you may have to colour combinations that you were told as a child do not 'go' together: blue and green, red and pink or whatever. Although it is true that certain colours do not help each other much, the quantities of each colour and the way they are combined are normally crucial factors. You will get a completely different effect from using a thin stripe of a contrasting colour, for example, than from using equal-sized blocks of colour.

Richly patterned fabric can give some good ideas for colour schemes if you use a couple of the colours, or tones of them, employed in the pattern. Equally, patterned china is another source of inspiration, and today's ceramic artists are using colour in increasingly bold and brilliant combinations.

Different cultures have favoured specific colours, the pigment often being found locally, hence the popularity of that particular shade. The Mexican earth shades of rich terracotta combined with a cool, bright light blue, or emerald green with yellow ochre, for example, are worth copying. Be careful, however, not to use these bright colours in ways that will make them dominate a colour scheme to the extent that it becomes hard to live with happily. They work better when used to pick out small items of furniture, panels, friezes or dados, with a lighter tone of the same or contrasting shade for larger areas.

Painters in the sixteenth century ground up their own pigments to make the paints, and some of them were so well-made that their colours remain true and unfaded even today. Early alchemists discovered many of the different pigments and over the centuries this repertoire has increased.

It is often rightly said that nature never makes a mistake as far as colour is concerned. There are no clashes in nature. It is also true that when you are using artificially created colours, you can create far less harmonious combinations. If you looked, for example, at vegetable-dyed wools, you could take any colours that you chose, put them together, and have an instantly attractive effect.

The harshness of chemical colours can produce some jarring contrasts and in terms of home decoration you would be wise to steer clear of very highly saturated or acidic-looking colours. They are hard to live with and do not marry easily with other colours.

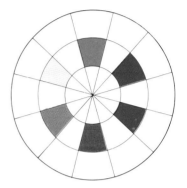

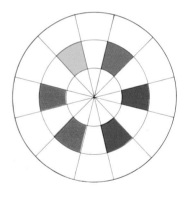

The top wheel shows the three primary colours: yellow, red and blue, and the colours that these primaries make when mixed together in equal quantities. The green is half and half yellow and blue, the orange is half and half red and yellow and the violet is half and half blue and red. The bottom wheel shows the different tones that occur when these mixed colours have more of one colour than of another, giving reddish orange, a yellow orange, a yellow green, a blue green, a bluey mauve and a reddish mauve.

An old blackwork pattern, popularly used for embroidered bed hangings in the seventeenth century, has been used to decorate a wall freehand in indigo, a nice touch being the way the design incorporates the radiator, which helps to disguise this slightly anachronistic fixture. The pelmet area of the cream chintz bedhangings have been stencilled in soft blues and greens.

COLOUR EFFECTS WITH PAINT

MANY BOOKS on interior decorating are full of wonderful pictures of paint effects, but give you no clue as to how difficult these are to reproduce, or how long this may take you. Watching an experienced decorator at work, I am always impressed by their skill and, above all, by their confidence. Part of it, I have to say, is their ability to make the right colour choices. You may well find it relatively easy to master the techniques of sponging (see page 64) for example, but the problem comes when you have to decide on the colours for it. The expert unerringly picks a base coat and a top glaze that produce a wonderfully rich effect. My first efforts were an unmitigated disaster. I sponged pale grey over quite a strong yellow, which gave the less than inspiring result of looking as though the walls were extremely dirty!

Left   This attic corner features a trompe-l'oeil *dovecote, complete with a stuffed dove on a perch in front of it for verisimilitude. The walls have been colour-washed in a soft sea-green while the beams have been antiqued in off-white.*

Opposite   Brilliant blues and yellows, combined with dusty pink, create a Matisse-like effect in this corner, the colour scheme picking up the combination of colours used for the decorated china pedestal. Strong, fully saturated colours work well when contrasted like this. If you lack the skill to paint freehand, as this has been, then create the same effect using printing blocks or rubber stamps.

19

This shows the room in which the trompe-l'oeil *detail, overleaf, appears. Among the interesting paint effects used are the marbled bedposts on the four-poster and the Moroccan tile effect painted on the small chest at the foot of the bed. The stone floor has also been painted. Provided it is well sealed after painting, even hardboard can make a successful floor covering.*

A pale base coat, with a darker glaze over the top, usually gives the best effect. Two different glaze colours, although more time-consuming, often look better than one.

Practise first on card to find the combinations of colours that produce the result you are after, and then leave it for a few days while you assimilate the effect and decide whether or not you can live with it. This is critically important in a time-consuming technique that is also difficult. Marbling your walls really beautifully is absolutely pointless if you do not like the overall effect in large areas! If you do not, try out your newly discovered technique on a small piece of furniture instead, which might anyway have been a better starting point.

FASHIONS IN DECORATION

WITHOUT GIVING a lengthy description of decorative styles, suffice it to say that through the centuries it has from time to time been fashionable to revive styles of bygone periods. Very little in interior decoration is actually new.

Although the history of paint effects is long – witness the first cave paintings in Lascaux in the Dordogne – their heyday in interior decoration probably began in the late seventeenth century as grand country houses like Dyrham Park and Belton House bear witness. In the nineteenth and early twentieth centuries the Victorian and Edwardian penchant for surface pattern, accompanied by a desire to parade the trappings of wealth, ensured the popularity of illusory paint effects, such as copying leather, marble or wood. The introduction of printed textiles and wallpapers had reduced the former need for hand-blocked or stencilled designs on walls and fabric, but the urge to decorate any available surface was so strong that craftsmen painters and decorators were always being called upon to create imitation marble pillars or japanned furniture. Découpage – the art of cutting out patterns from paper and sticking them to a surface before varnishing it – was immensely popular as a pastime for gently born women in the nineteenth century.

Walls provided an area for surface decoration of all kinds, and in many ordinary houses the wooden panelling of the homes of the well-to-do was imitated using the newly patented lincrusta and anaglypta raised wallpapers, which were then painted to look like wood or embossed leather.

The Arts and Crafts movement, under the leadership of William Morris, saw a return to the tradition of the artist craftsmen of medieval times. The wonderfully rich colours of the natural dyes used in their textiles, and the intricately wrought patterns, for which nature provided the inspiration in the form of birds, beasts, flowers and fruit, are emblematic of the movement. Although the founders of the movement set themselves against the soul-destroying effects of mechanization, it was ironically this same mechanization that later brought Morris's designs, in mass-produced form, to the population at large.

It was only with the advent of minimalism in the years before the Second World War that the interest in surface decoration declined. It lay in the doldrums until the late 1950s when John Fowler (of Colefax and Fowler) reintroduced it. Post-modern architecture and design also witnessed a return to decoration, and with it a growing interest in the techniques of paint effects.

Anyone seriously interested in interior decoration should certainly take the time to read a good history of the subject, such as Peter Thornton's

Authentic Decor: the domestic interior 1620–1920. This not only traces the changes in fashion over a 300-year period, but gives endless ideas for decorative schemes for bedrooms and bathrooms, as well as showing, with its great wealth of colour plates, the colour schemes favoured in different periods.

BEDROOMS

Bedrooms, or bedchambers as they were once called, are a relatively modern concept. In the early part of the Middle Ages even the wealthy did not have separate bedrooms. All the members of the household lived and slept in one room, heated by a central fire which had no chimney – just a hole in the roof.

With the architectural advance of the built chimney, it became possible to divide the living space into separate rooms, and the concept of the bedroom was born. The room contained little else besides the bed, which, in the houses of the well-to-do, was often a sumptuous affair. The four-poster, however, had an entirely practical purpose in those days. The supports afforded a place from which thick drapes could be hung to keep out the cold. The richer people were, the more elaborate the drapery, as a visit to a museum such as the Victoria and Albert in London quickly reveals, with some remarkable examples complete with ornate gold embroidery and crewelwork or fantastic beasts and birds. In humbler homes, people had to make do with simple board beds and straw mattresses in alcoves, with perhaps a curtain hung across to provide some privacy. Otherwise master, mistress, children and servants shared the same sleeping quarters.

By the seventeenth century the bedroom had become a major feature of the house, reaching its apogee a century later when it was used as a room for entertaining as well as for sleeping. Ladies in the eighteenth century received visitors in the bedroom, holding court from luxurious four-posters. In France, the decoration of the bedroom during this period was in the true rococo style, with swags, ribbons and bows proliferating, the walls hung with expensive silks imported from China.

Advances in the glass-making industry in the same century meant that windows became larger, and pull-up curtains were introduced which allowed the light to be let in or excluded at will. Simpler versions of today's festoon and Austrian blinds, they were operated by being pulled up in their entirety on a simple cord and pulley system.

With the advent of the industrial revolution, and the rise in the merchant classes, it became the vogue to display new-found wealth as overtly as possible. A decorative style was spawned in which ornament was all. Bedrooms became cluttered, stuffed with richly upholstered daybeds and chairs, pictures and plants on jardinières. The cotton mills were churning out vast quantities of fine cotton cloth, both patterned and plain. Advances in textile printing techniques, pioneered in France in the Toile de Jouy factories south-west of Paris, brought patterned fabrics to within the reach of a larger swathe of the population.

Opposite An early eighteenth-century Swedish bedroom. The wooden walls and ceiling would have been brightly painted, forming a lively setting for the jauntily swagged blue-and-white bed hangings.

This small attic bedroom has an attractively stencilled and antiqued chest of drawers. A pale cream paint has been used over brown, and rubbed back to allow the undercoat to show through, to give it an aged appearance. Waxing after painting with a dark wax also helps to age paintwork artificially. Keeping the stencilled colours very soft so that they blend and tone also helps to give the piece an authentically old appearance.

The social changes caused by the First World War, with votes and more varied employment for women, and far fewer domestic servants, brought the romanticism of the late nineteenth century to an end. A new mood swept through design and architecture: concrete, glass and plastic became the favoured materials, and design became functional, minimalist and severe. Central heating became more usual, fireplaces were removed, kitchens streamlined, gadgets proliferated. By the middle of the twentieth century, abstract patterns, strong colours and simple outlines were the order of the day, and clutter, ornament and decoration were firmly out of fashion.

In the last decade, there has been a swing back to a more natural, romantic look, and ethnic influences have also become increasingly evident, design drawing on a variety of cultures and sources for inspiration. In decorating terms, this has led to a greater desire to 'personalize' interiors, with hand-painted finishes, much greater use of pattern and warmer, richer colours, as decorative paint techniques are the ideal medium in which to express this return to individuality, colour and expression.

BATHROOMS

Although the Romans and Egyptians were enthusiastic bathers, cleanliness in medieval Europe was not deemed second to godliness. By the sixteenth century, however, there was a growing realization that hygiene contributed to health, and the rich took baths occasionally, in tubs filled by servants. The poorer made do, if they washed much at all, with a bucket of cold water.

By the seventeenth century interest in personal hygiene had resulted in bathrooms being installed in some private houses, but the plumbing was primitive and the drainage non-existent. An early example of an eighteenth-century Florentine bathroom in the Italian *Magazzino di Mobilia* depicts an

This carefully recreated medieval bathroom – the Queen's Bathroom – at Leeds Castle, Kent, features a fabric-draped bath and rich wall hangings. As well as being historically authentic, the effect is at once stylish and charming.

elaborate pedestal-legged bath surmounted by a canopy of green silk. The water issues out of twin lion-head masks fixed into the wall, but the bath had to be drained by hand.

Although water closets had been invented about a hundred years earlier in England (the euphemistic 'loo' is a corruption of the French term *lieu à l'anglaise*, the name given to the water closet), they were hardly commonplace even in the eighteenth century. Chatsworth, the seat of the Dukes of Devonshire, however, is recorded as having 10 water closets installed as early as the 1690s.

Those houses that did have baths treated them in the grand manner, positioning them in the centre of the room, and giving them the same tent-like canopy falling from a central crown that was the fashion for beds at the time. This canopy served a dual purpose: it kept draughts out and the steam in, making the bath into an early form of sauna. It also presumably offered the bather some privacy from the army of servants marching about with towels and hot water!

Even by the mid-nineteenth century, bathrooms were still very much a luxury and there was no form of public sewage system. In cities, it was the job of nightmen to cart away the slops. As late as the 1840s, the River Thames in London was still an open sewer and the first public lavatories were not installed until the late 1880s.

By the middle of the twentieth century, bathrooms were the rule but it has taken even longer to bring people back to an appreciation of the luxury and relaxation of bathing, with the introduction of showers, whirlpool baths, hot tubs and saunas.

Bathrooms today are seen as an essential part of civilized living, and with the advent of small-bore pipework which means that they no longer have to be plumbed close to an outside wall, ensuite bathrooms for each bedroom have become a common feature of many houses and flats.

Opposite   Delicately tinted walls, painted in a technique that blends sponging with marbling, in soft pinks, greens and golds, give a classical feel to this bathroom, while the colour scheme stops it from looking cold. Even the floor has been painted, an imitation marble, created by using a dark undercoat, with a light beige paint over the top, the grouting picked out in dark terracotta.

PLANNING THE WORK

THIS PART of the book covers the practical elements that need to be considered when decorating, for both bedrooms and bathrooms, and the fundamental techniques involved, including preparation, the constituent ingredients of paint, and the basic paint techniques.

Without a carefully planned and meticulously executed approach, any decoration scheme, no matter how creatively conceived, will founder. It is also impossible to apply the more complex broken paint effects successfully to badly prepared or painted surfaces.

BEDROOMS

Opposite Simplicity, in the form of plain white painted walls, can often be the best solution, particularly where, as here, the furniture is antique dark oak. White linen and lace bed-hangings and cream linen covers complete the cool effect.

U NLESS YOU are unwell or especially indolent, you are unlikely to spend as many of your waking hours in your bedroom as in other rooms. Your prime considerations when it comes to decorating your bedroom are your own psychological make-up and the lifestyle you lead.

For most people, the décor of the bedroom must be sympathetic. It is not the place to experiment with avant garde designs or particularly strident colour schemes, partly because staring at the results on the nights when sleep fails to come may well drive you mad! That does not mean, however, that deep, rich colours or even quite exciting colour contrasts should not be used, but you should, at least, be aware of the possible consequences.

In most double bedrooms, the bed or beds will fill a large amount of the available space and, therefore, much of the decorative surface, so it is wise also to consider the covers, hangings, if any, and bedlinen when you plan a colour scheme for the room.

A bed with simple white or neutral linen and covers will fit into most colour schemes, but you may well have a beautiful antique patchwork quilt or particularly bold, geometric bed covers. If you know that you do not want to change these, then use their colours as a starting point for any colour scheme for the other surfaces, perhaps picking out one of the key colours to paint skirting boards, picture rails or cornices.

As far as individual touches are concerned, there is no reason why you have to stop at painting the surfaces and furniture in the bedroom. Fabrics, these days, can also be successfully painted using relatively simple techniques. Do-it-yourself fabric painting is an inexpensive way of creating an individual feeling for a room, since you can buy the cheapest unbleached calico on which to make your mark. Bed-hangings and covers, roller and roman blinds, wall panels and lampshades are all candidates for fabric painting (see page 121).

PLANNING THE BEDROOM

Before you start designing, or redesigning, a bedroom, you need to ask yourself some practical questions. The first of these is: what do you use the room for? This might appear to invite some silly answers, but as a famous designer once said, form follows function. In other words, everything must be designed with a specific purpose in mind.

The bedroom can be used in different ways. For some of us, it is simply a comfortable place to sleep; for others, it is a study and office as well; for yet others, it is close to being a sanctuary – a private and very personal space.

You might therefore start by considering whether you are sleeping in the right room. Do you really need the largest room in the house, or would your child or children be better off with it, so that they, and their friends, can liberate the living room? Which way does the room face? If you like to sleep late, an east-facing bedroom, or one that looks on to a noisy street, can be a problem. Children normally are up fairly early, so early morning light is unlikely to bother them that much. If necessary, you can cut out the light with shutters or heavily interlined curtains.

How much storage space do you have in the bedroom and is it the right shape and size for the objects you want to put away? Can you get at your clothes quickly and easily in the mornings? Are the items you use less often, or not for considerable periods of time – such as winter clothes in summer – stored away in the less accessible places and the items you need every day kept where you can get at them easily?

The plan shows how both the double bedroom and the single can have access to the bathroom. Adequate space has been allowed for opening the cupboard doors easily.

People's storage needs are very personal. Some of us make do with very little, and others seem to collect enough junk to start a second-hand shop. Very few of the pictures you see in magazines and books show the average kind of clutter that most people have in their houses – it has been swept under the bed or behind the sofa for the photographer, one assumes – but if you want to keep your bedroom looking like a film set, then cupboard space, and lots of it, is the only solution.

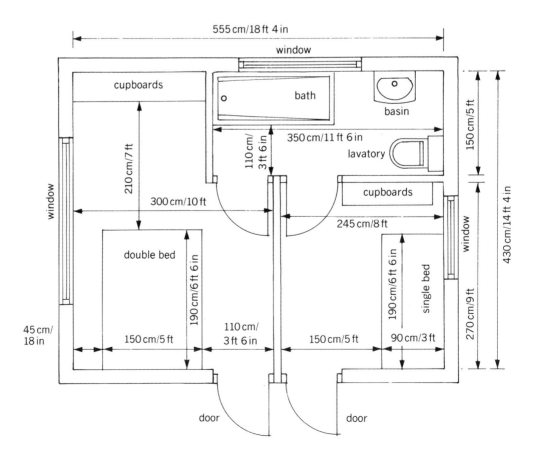

Some of the most attractive cupboards have been tailor-made to fit the odd nooks and crannies you find in the majority of houses, and although it is expensive to get a carpenter to make cupboards for you, this can often be worth the outlay provided you have already considered what you are going to store in them. The wood does not need to be particularly expensive, so long as it is solid and does not warp, because there are so many interesting paint effects you can use to decorate cupboards. In fact, they provide you with a wonderful opportunity to exercise your paint effect skills.

Another point to consider is whether you are being ruthless enough with the stuff you do store away. How often do you have a turn-out?

Do not forget when organizing a bedroom that you need a certain amount of space to get round the bed to make it. It is most infuriating having to struggle in a room in which the bed takes up more of the floor space than it should. If you have a flat with a large living room and a small bedroom, you might seriously consider sleeping in the living area, and turning the bedroom into a study or dining room. Investing money in an attractive Empire-style bed which doubles as a sofa, and which you can put in the living room, may be much more comfortable than two of you trying to cope with a double bed pushed against one wall, so that one of you has always to climb over the other to get in and out.

Another solution might be to split a large living room into a sitting and a sleeping area with screens, freeing a small bedroom for other purposes.

In Japanese culture, it is still the norm to have a movable bed – a cotton futon that can be simply rolled up in the morning and unrolled at night. There is much to be said for this simple way of living in today's rather overcrowded conditions, because it frees you to use the space in whatever manner you like, rather than parcelling it up into smaller spaces with specific functions. The current fashion for futons in the West is probably due at least in part to the flexibility that this kind of sleeping arrangements offers.

COLOUR IN THE BEDROOM

The choice of colours is bound to be personal but since the bedroom, if it has a double bed in it, is going to be largely dominated by that bed, it is worth thinking about the colour scheme as a united concept. In other words, do not plan the paint effects for the walls, ceiling and furniture without thinking what you are going to do about the bed linen and bed covers.

Carefully co-ordinated schemes tend to assume that you have a great deal of money and can simply whizz out and buy sets of bedlinen to match whatever new paint scheme you are planning. The bedlinen is probably rather more expensive than the paint, so if your budget is limited, work your scheme around the colours and pattern of the linen you already have, or alternatively buy a cover which you can throw over the whole bed. There are some good, and inexpensive, Indian cotton throws that are ideal for this purpose, and a few cushions, in colours to match the new scheme, will give the room a lift without breaking the bank.

Rich deep green oil-based paint has been combined with dark green bed-hangings, curtains and covers, lined and contrasted with dark red damask, and coupled with crisp white linen to create a sumptuous Renaissance feel to this bedroom. The bed-hangings are a modern version of the half-tester, in which the drapes fall from the wall above the bed head.

Choosing colours again depends to a large extent on how you use the bedroom. If it is limited to night-time use, there is nothing to stop you from going for something rich, dark and cosy-looking, using deeper colours than you might choose to do in the rest of the house. If, however, you want to use the bedroom as a study as well as a sleeping area, it might be better to pick a more neutral scheme.

I have a great dislike of very strong-coloured schemes in a bedroom, precisely because it is likely to be the one place in the house where you may get time to contemplate. You do not really want to have your thoughts deflected by very vibrant colours or a dominant colour scheme. If you want a room to relax in, opt for something peaceful and fairly neutral, hopefully without being boring.

A delicately stencilled border, or some attractively painted cupboards or furniture, seems to be the ideal choice for bedrooms, perhaps even given a deliberately 'aged' appearance. To me, too, the warmer colours – apricots, warm creams, beiges and slightly off pinks – seem to suit bedrooms more than the cooler blues and greens. If you do want to use rich strong colours, they could be used over small areas, and offset with white to give them a lift.

Fabric can also do a lot to soften and offset a cool-looking room, but do not fall into the trap of turning the room into something resembling a pair of old-fashioned bloomers, with billowing Austrian blinds, ruched fabric over the bed and frilly cushions.

STUDIOS

Studios, or bedsitting rooms as they are less attractively called, require careful thought in terms of interior decoration as a variety of functions are being carried on in one room. In planning a colour scheme you will need to be aware of your daytime and night-time needs.

Living in one room can make you feel both cramped and claustrophobic, unless it happens to be a huge room with a high ceiling. If you are lucky enough to have such a room, you have the option of moving the bed or bedroom area to a mezzanine level, which immediately increases the usable space. There are a variety of methods of raising the bed, depending on the available room height. Where this is not particularly great, a partially raised system with shelving or desk space underneath can be incorporated. In rooms with really high ceilings, a gallery bedroom can be constructed.

In a fairly small area, it pays to choose pale colours which visually enlarge the available space, limiting strong colours to the furnishings or small areas, such as dados or panels. Any of the broken colour painting techniques (see pages 63–79) can be used successfully, but again it pays to opt for a colour scheme where the base coat and the glaze are not too dissimilar in hue.

The bed itself can either be a convertible type, such as a sofa bed (although very few seem to be comfortable enough to sleep on regularly) or futon (which you do get used to in time). Alternatively, if you want to divide the functions, the bed and sleeping area can be separated from the rest of the room using free-standing furniture, floor-to-ceiling shelving, blinds or free-standing screens. The blinds and screens can be painted, if you wish, using some of the techniques outlined in this book. Even tall plants, such as palms, dracaenas or the small-leafed fig, *Ficus benjaminus*, can be used as a partial screen.

NURSERIES AND CHILDREN'S ROOMS

Adults do not normally scribble on the walls or chuck their drinks on the floor, but since all small children are likely to go in for either or both of these activities, any decoration scheme for a child's room needs to be practical.

The main element required is flexibility. As children grow, their needs change and these should be catered for with the minimum of fuss and expense. Most of the stuff that they collect – toys, books, their own artwork – is attractive in its own right, so the best solution is to have a fairly simple paint scheme, in which the artefacts become the focal point. For this reason, lots of

pinboard space and shelving are essential. Painted furniture that has been properly varnished is ideal, because it can be wiped clean easily.

It is not worth spending hours and hours on some extremely time-consuming paint technique. The children will not appreciate it. Most of the wall space will end up covered with posters, and I have yet to find a method of putting posters up on a wall that does not leave an unpleasant mark when they are discarded or exchanged for some other piece of decoration.

For toddlers, it is well worth considering painting the area up to the dado with some easily washable surface, since small black handprints seem to mushroom overnight. The landing and staircase need the same treatment!

It is sensible to have plenty of open and closed storage space as well, since children seem to accumulate enough toys, after several Christmases and birthdays, to open a superstore. If you do not want their small friends to remove the wheels of the very expensive model Ferrari Grandad gave them for Christmas, you need somewhere to put any toys with removable pieces out of sight and out of reach.

When planning a child's bedroom remember it should be child-centred, not parent-centred. It is not you who has to live in and sleep in it, so do not impose your taste on your child. There is an inherent danger, however, in giving the child too much freedom of choice. When I asked my seven-year-old what colour he wanted to have his bedroom painted, he insisted on black! It took a great deal of persuasion to get him to relinquish this idea. Perhaps he would have enjoyed it. If your child fancies the prospect, there is nothing to stop him or her having a go at painting their own roller blind or a mural on the wall, with a bit of help from you.

Safety is of course an important factor with small children. Make sure no material you use in their bedroom is in any way toxic, or can be peeled off and chewed or swallowed.

GUEST ROOMS

In most houses, space is at a premium so it is important to make the best possible use of every room. A guest room that doubles as an office or study is usually the best solution, and a futon, which acts as a sofa during the day and a double bed at night, is an ideal choice. Don't forget that you will need somewhere to store the spare bedding (some sofa beds have drawers fitted underneath for this purpose) and also some spare shelving, and hanging space, for any guests' clothes and personal belongings.

Children's bedrooms are often best decorated in fairly simple, neutral schemes, with the interest added in the form of stencilled or découpaged images. Here the two nursery chairs have been découpaged. Nursery story motifs can be cut out and transferred using this technique (see page 109).

BATHROOMS

Opposite This bathroom has a wonderfully soft finish, with sponged walls in misty mauve and pink, the window frame and cupboard picked out in plain lavender. The sides of the roll-topped, claw-footed bath have been painted deep blue, with a pale pink water lily motif painted freehand. A muslin curtain draped over a pole completes the romantic effect.

The plan shows how the sanitary fittings can be positioned in quite a small bathroom.

A COLD, uninviting bathroom can let down an otherwise pleasant house or flat. For many of us, having a bath or shower is one of the best ways of unwinding when we are tired or stressed, and it is always worthwhile spending a little extra time, and money on the decoration scheme for the bathroom.

Nothing, however, will work well for you if the bathroom is badly planned already: if the lavatory is too close to the bath or basin, or behind the door, and if there is no place provided for towels and the general paraphernalia one needs. Do remember that the sanitary fittings are going to be there for some time, and if they need replacing, buy decent quality ones that will last, and make sure the taps and other fittings are solid and well-constructed.

Not that long ago, bathrooms were given a pretty functional treatment, and they certainly were not really places to linger in. Recently, a more sybaritic view of the bathroom has held sway, and some people have chosen to rearrange their houses, turning a much larger bedroom into a bathroom, with perhaps a large Victorian bath holding pride of place in the centre of a room

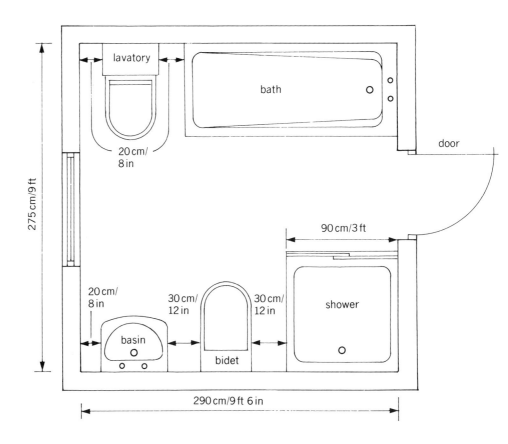

that looks more like a drawing room than a bathroom. If you have a lot of money, and a house with a lot of space, this is certainly attractive, but for most people, pressure on space is too great, and the solution lies in making the most of what you have already got.

In terms of decoration, much depends on how you live. A busy bachelor or career woman, rushing in to shower before going out for the evening, would probably find a simple, streamlined bathroom ideal. Families with small children, where everybody seems to end up in the bathroom together, need a different approach. If their existing bathroom is very small, it may well be worth considering the outlay of turning a spare room into a larger bathroom, or at least turning the space under the stairs into a shower/cloakroom.

A separate lavatory is essential if there are more than two of you in the house, unless you are very liberal-minded about possibly having no privacy.

Although practical considerations are very necessary in the bathroom, with so much water splashing about, it is important, too, that it does not become overly clinical in an effort to protect it against spills and stains. Well-painted wood can be as waterproof as any other material, but you do need to make sure that any joins between surfaces are properly sealed and waterproofed. Wood panelling up to dado level can be just as practical as tiling, and rather more warm and inviting-looking.

In recent years, white has come back into fashion for sanitary fittings. It has two distinct advantages: it is cheaper than coloured ware, and it goes with almost any colour scheme you care to choose. Whether it will go out of fashion again remains to be seen. For me, it has never been out of fashion. I always disliked coloured suites, and the ones I preferred were those Edwardian-looking ones, now so much in vogue, that you found in old country houses, all made, I think, by one well-known manufacturer. The lavatory had a proper overhead cistern with a satisfying chain that you could pull. With many modern suites, the flush mechanism is so cunningly designed that it takes you a few minutes in a strange bathroom to find it!

Bathroom fittings have a nasty habit of coming away from the wall if lent on or if your hefty teenager decides to wash his feet in the handbasin. Make sure you use a recognized plumber and that all the fittings are correctly plumbed in. Do not make the mistake of enclosing the sides of the bath so permanently that when something goes wrong with the plumbing, the plumber cannot get to it without tearing all the covering down. Jointed, removable panels are the answer. You do not have to box in all the plumbing. You can make a feature of it, if you like, painting it perhaps in a different colour or leaving it in its natural copper.

Crisp and clean, without looking clinical, this periwinkle blue and white bathroom has been designed around the stained glass insets in the window. Pine cupboards, an old pine towel rail and wood-mounted prints, help to soften the formality of the scheme which has an almost sculptural quality.

Since washing in hot water generates a lot of steam, ventilation is important in the bathroom if condensation is not going to ruin the paintwork. The window, if there is one, must be capable of being opened, and if the bathroom has no exterior window, a fan-assisted air vent leading to an exterior wall will be needed.

In very small bathrooms, it is not essential to have a bath fitted. You can opt for a shower unit instead or do what many continentals do, install a half-bath. Deeper than a standard bath, these are made in various sizes, and a shower unit can be incorporated. Unfortunately, like anything which is not standard, they cost more!

WALLS

Most people prefer to cover the areas surrounding the bath and basin with tiles because they provide a suitably waterproof surface. Although all the wall surface can be tiled, it presents a rather clinical appearance which is not to everyone's taste. Half-tiling the walls is a good compromise.

If, like me, you prefer rather more sympathetic-looking bathrooms, then stencilling (see page 105) provides an effective method of 'personalizing' a rather austere bathroom.

Colour also plays a big part in the atmosphere you create. Traditionally, people opt for cool colours in bathrooms, with the associations these have with water. Although this is pleasant in hot climates, it is not such an attractive proposition in the grip of an arctic winter. Warmer terracottas, yellows and apricots, especially contrasting with white bathroom fittings, seem to offer a cosier, more relaxed environment. Deep rich colours can also be used very successfully in bathrooms, especially when combined with imitation dark wood-graining on bath panels, cupboards, skirtings and doors.

Pattern is something to be a little careful about in bathrooms. In small areas, it can be overwhelming and too many ready-made bathroom accessories have patterns comprising hackneyed sea or water imagery – shells, ducks or boats being the most popular. Go for something a bit different in the way of pattern if you do want to keep to the 'water' theme. Maybe a découpage Roman bath-style frieze, with imitation sandstone walls. Be careful how you mix pattern, and do not mix the imagery.

The main aim in the bathroom is to ensure that the paintwork is water-resistant, and if you do not want the paint to crack or peel, you will probably have to give any paint effect you choose a couple of coats of matt, polyurethane varnish to waterproof and seal it.

FLOORS

Although ceramic tiles are the most practical solution for the bathroom floor, they are not particularly welcoming or warm to the feet. Parquet or wood boards are much warmer; they can be bleached by liming, or stained in various patterns, or painted with floor paints, and then sealed with several coats of varnish for durability.

Bathroom floors, being fairly small, are ideal places to experiment with perhaps a stencilled border pattern on the floor. You can use wood stains for this purpose, which now come in a range of colours as well as traditional wood colours, or any of the products normally used for stencilling (see page 102), preferably in fairly soft colours that tone well with the colour of the boards or are diluted sufficiently to allow the wood colour to show through. Whatever medium you use, the floor will have to be properly sealed afterwards with sufficient coats of varnish to make it water-resistant and wearproof.

Cork is also warm but wears quickly, and tends to lift if a lot of water is splashed over it. Heavy-duty linoleum is also warmer than ceramic tiles, and some very good colours and patterns can now be found. Existing cork and linoleum can be painted and sealed to give them a new lease of life.

FIXTURES AND FITTINGS

The bath surround, or the outside of the bath itself, and any cupboards or wooden panelling in the bathroom are ideal places to experiment with different paint techniques. The false effects of marbling and wood-graining come into their own in the bathroom, at half the cost of the real thing. It is important to have a theme in mind, and to match the techniques to this. Do not mix styles, periods and materials with abandon unless you are very sure of your 'eye'. Go for a look: Biedermeier with its pale golden polished wood, straight classical with cool marble, or homespun country with bleached wood, pale stencils and soft pastel colours.

FABRICS

Bathroom shower curtains and blinds or curtains can also be given the paint treatment. Every time I have looked for shower curtains, I have been singularly unimpressed with the choice unless you want to pay a fortune. If in doubt, settle for plain white and stencil your own pattern on it. Borders can be painted on blinds or curtains – even very simple stripes or geometric patterns look extremely effective if you make a good colour choice, and can pick up a colour used in a small area elsewhere in the room.

CLOAKROOMS AND LAVATORIES

If you have a house with a second lavatory or downstairs cloakroom (and quite often the space underneath the stairs in a suburban semi can be used for this purpose, although of course you do then lose a lot of useful storage space), it is the ideal place to practice your first attempts at decorative paint finishes. For a start, the area is usually very small and therefore within the beginner's grasp, as the most difficult aspect of broken paint effects is achieving an even finish over a large area.

MIXING COLOURS

HALF THE fun of decorative painting lies in mixing your own colours. For some reason, many people are very nervous of doing so, but provided you proceed systematically, you are unlikely to make any really expensive mistakes.

The best way is to start with a base colour, and then add colour to it little by little. Work from pale to dark, rather than the reverse. Keep notes of the colours and quantities added as you mix, so that when you succeed in getting the colour you want, you can repeat the formula. Prepare some sample boards using hardboard or thick card, primed to prevent the paint soaking into it. You can paint an area of card about 30 cm/12 inches square and prop it up in the room you plan to decorate to assess the effect.

The primary colours are red, yellow and blue – any other colour is simply a mixture of these. When buying artists' colours with which to tint paint, you could stick to these three basic colours, with white or black for tone, but it is easier for you if you have a slightly wider range at your disposal. A good basic palette of artists' colours would be burnt and raw umber, burnt and raw sienna, medium chrome yellow, red oxide, cadmium red, veridian and ultramarine blue. These colours can be bought in oil or acylic paints, depending on the base with which they are to be mixed. Universal stainers can also be used but the colour range is more limited.

COMPOSITION OF PAINT

In order to achieve the right effects when using broken paint techniques, it helps to know a little bit about the composition of paint. Although the paint industry is constantly carrying out research to discover better mixtures and media for the paint, the fundamental recipe has not changed that much since paint was first invented. However, as a result of innovations in paint manufacture, some of the previous golden rules have now altered.

The original colouring agent was pigment, a natural substance found in varying forms, but primarily geological in origin. The medium in which the colour, or pigment, is carried has varied over the centuries, from linseed oil or turpentine to oil or whiting (a form of chalk), depending on whether the paint is oil- or water-based.

Modern paints, which come in a range of sheen finishes, from flat matt to high gloss, are now being produced with an acrylic base as well. These can be used quite successfully in paint finishes, but the drying time is much shorter, which means that what is known as the 'wet edge' does not last as long, making it harder to complete the work before the paint dries. Acrylic-based paints have the huge advantage that they can be thinned with water, and the brushes can therefore also be cleaned in water, and it is easier to wipe up spills. However, for some of the techniques you would have to work with a partner, as otherwise the paint would dry before you could finish the job. Also, the finished effect is not as translucent as that achieved with oil-based paint.

One of the first points to remember is that oil and water do not mix. While it is possible to cover a water-based paint with an oil-based one, the reverse simply does not work. Emulsion paint will not adhere to gloss paint unless the latter has been sanded first. Nor can you combine oil and water in any kind of medium; it simply separates out.

Equally, surfaces will absorb oil unless previously primed, so a standard-type oil-based paint cannot normally be applied direct to an unprimed surface, although paint manufacturers have now brought out a range of oil-based paints that can be applied direct to an unprimed surface, thereby confusing you further!

Citrus yellow and shades of blue have been used to create an unusual but very successful colour scheme in this attic bedroom. Repeating the colours in different parts of the room – the blue of the bedhead is echoed in the colour of the skirting boards, while the colour-washed wood-panelled walls are a paler tone of the ceiling – helps to unify the disparate, contrasting colours.

Many of the ingredients used in paint effects have their origins in the world of fine art, and the best range of artists' oils and acrylics will be found in artists' supply shops rather than in hardware stores.

MAKING GLAZES

Most of the paint techniques consist of a base coat with a glaze over the top which is worked in some form – with brushes, rags or combs – to create a mottled or textured effect. The success of this depends on the glaze being thin (the consistency of single cream) and fairly transparent so that the base coat shows through. It is this translucence that gives the effect its character. An eggshell base coat with an oil-based glaze will give a more sheeny finish, which many people prefer. Equally, an emulsion base coat with an acrylic-based glaze will be more matt and even in appearance (although this is not always an option, because the acrylic glaze dries too fast for more complex techniques such as stippling).

Glaze recipes are based on a transparent medium, which is tinted and thinned to suit the requirements of specific effects. The medium can be bought ready-made at any good paint store (it is often called scumble), but you can make it up yourself if you wish. An oil-based glaze is made from equal parts of boiled linseed oil and turpentine, with the addition of a small amount of driers (also known as siccatives) to speed up the drying time. Without the driers, the glaze could take several days to dry thoroughly. Once the medium is made up, it can be further thinned (with turpentine or water, as appropriate) to suit the paint effect you are engaged on. The normal ratio is to add about 20 per cent thinner to the glaze.

A range of acrylic-based glazes is now widely available. They are mixed with water and used over vinyl silk, and are, owing to the water base, less smelly to use than oil-based glazes. The finish is, however, flatter in appearance and less luminous.

To colour the glaze you can use acrylics (for water-based glazes) or artists' oils (for oil-based glazes). Mix the oils with a little turpentine first before adding to the glaze. Add very sparingly – surprisingly little is needed to darken the glaze, and it looks even darker when out of the tin. Universal stainers (which can be used to tint either oil- or water-based glazes) are obtainable, but the range of colours is not as extensive. Powder paints can also be used to tint both types of glaze. Always test your colours on a piece of board first, and keep a note of the proportions you used, so that you can make up another batch if and when needed. It helps to keep a notebook with a blob of the final colour, and the recipe for it. This is particularly important when you are mixing several colours to achieve the final result.

Another bold scheme juxtaposes colour and pattern to make its impact. Although these walls have been painted freehand by an artist, you could imitate the effect using stencils or rubber stamps.

PREPARING TO PAINT

Creating marbled effects successfully is the hallmark of the decorative paint finish expert. It takes patience and perseverance to achieve but it is the ideal technique to use in bathrooms since real marble is too dear for most people. The colour and pattern of the real marble tiled floor have been imitated on the walls and fittings in this cloakroom.

P AINT CAN be applied to most surfaces, provided they are properly prepared first. In the case of existing paintwork that is in reasonable condition, it will probably only need to be thoroughly vacuumed. Areas of paintwork that are very dirty or greasy will need to be cleaned with a brush or large sponge and some detergent before being painted. Rinse any detergent off completely before starting to paint.

Any cracks in the plaster should be filled first (see box). Bumps or lumps can be sanded smooth. Check with your local hardware store as to what grade of sanding paper to use for a specific job.

Surfaces that have not previously been painted will need priming first. There is a form of primer for every kind of surface you might want to paint, including metal, laminates, concrete, brick and even glass. If in doubt about the preparation and kind of primer to use on an unusual material, ask for advice in the local hardware shop. Stiff canvas can be primed with a primer made from five parts emulsion paint to two parts PVA. Ordinary fabric for painting needs no priming.

Primers come in three types: water-, oil- or alcohol-based. Your choice of primer depends on what finish you are planning to apply, as oil- and water-based paints can be applied over alcohol or water-based primers, but oil-based primers will have to be finished with oil-based paints.

An alcohol-based primer known as shellac is useful for many different paint finishes as it dries extremely quickly. It is, however, smelly and any spills will have to be removed with methylated spirits. It is particularly useful for sealing plaster and unpainted wood, making an effective knot sealer as well.

Some primers are very toxic and you will need to wear a mask so that you do not inhale the fumes. Read the manufacturer's instructions carefully, and make sure that you obey them.

FILLING CRACKS AND HOLES

It is a relatively simple matter these days to fill cracks and holes, since plaster filler comes ready-mixed in tubs and tubes. You will need a filling knife and a shavehook as well.

Scrape out the crack or hole to make sure you have a suitable edge to which the filler can adhere. Then wipe it clean with a sponge, before applying the filler, usually in a couple of coats at least, allowing each one to dry before the next is inserted. Overfill rather than under-fill any indentation, and then sand-smooth any bumps afterwards.

WORKING WITH PAINT

Try to be as systematic as possible when you work. Cover floors and furniture with dust-sheets, plastic sheeting or newspaper. Put the paint you are planning to use in a suitable container such as a roller tray or large bucket on a table covered in plastic sheeting. Paint stirrers, spare buckets and containers, and the brushes and tools you will be needing should also be laid out ready, with plenty of rags and the appropriate medium for wiping up any spills.

Wear overalls yourself, or old clothes, with gloves and a mask if dealing with substances that give off fumes. Make sure the area is kept well-ventilated but not draughty. Check that any ladders or steps you intend using are stable and will support your weight properly. Paint tins should be sealed carefully after use so that they are airtight, and stored away from heat or sunlight. Brushes should be cleaned after use and hung up to dry (see page 51).

Brushes

A GOOD workman never blames his tools, but if you buy cheap brushes, you certainly will! And with reason, too, because cheap brushes do not have sufficient bristles, or of a fine enough quality, for the paint to be applied smoothly.

The paint technique you choose determines the tools for the job. There is a wide range of specialist brushes available, but unless you are going to become seriously involved in paint effects, the expense is probably too great to be justified. There are certain basic tools that you should have.

You will need a good quality, large-sized decorator's brush for applying the base coat for most finishes. Feel the bristles and check that they are firm, flexible and full. Don't buy the cheapest, but price alone is not a guarantee of quality. You will also need various smaller, similarly good quality brushes for narrow areas. If you plan to varnish your paint effects, you will need a soft, full, varnishing brush, which you keep solely for that purpose.

Individual brushes are required for different techniques, such as a stiff-bristled brush for stippling, a very soft-bristled brush for smoothing out after a paint effect has been worked, and, for dragging, you should ideally use a special flogger, or long-bristled brush, for the best results. If you go in for stencilling with a brush, you will need a special brush, which is short and round with stubby, stiffish bristles. If the brush is too soft, the bristles will creep under the bridges of the stencil and spoil the image. If you decide to spray the stencils instead, then obviously you can dispense with the brush. For spattering or stippling over small areas you will need a stiff-bristled artist's brush, sometimes known as a fitch.

Opposite   This soft dusty blue complements the warm colour of the beams and the chest of drawers beautifully. Delicate stippling in toning shades of blue and grey gives the walls a matt appearance that works very well in this cottage-style setting, while the chest has been painted olive green, and antiqued.

CLEANING AND STORING BRUSHES

It is important to clean your brushes as soon as you have finished using them. Paint that has dried on the bristles is laborious to remove. If you are using water-based paints (including acrylics), you can wash the brushes out with ordinary soap and warm, not hot, water. Make sure you remove all the paint from the part where the bristles join the handle, and then rinse thoroughly and allow to dry naturally. Ideally, dry the brushes hanging, so that the air circulates around the bristles.

If you are using oil-based paints, you will have to clean the brushes with white spirit or a proprietary brush-cleaning fluid. When they are clean, rinse them in water and dry as before.

Varnish brushes will also need to be cleaned in the same way, depending on whether the varnish is oil or water-based.

Cotton Stockinette

Hog Hair Softener

Badger Hair Softener

Decorator's Brushes

Artist's Brushes

Spoons for Mixing

Natural Sponge

Mottler

Fitches

Gilder/ Varnish Brush

Indian Hog Hair Flogging Brush

Dragging Brush

Stencilling Brush

Stippling Brush

Metal Comb

THE MATERIALS

Paint for decorating, as opposed to art, is produced in two main forms: oil-based and water-based. The pigment in oil-based paint is fixed with linseed oil and thinned down with turpentine (white spirit), whereas in water-based paint it is fixed with acrylic resin and thinned with water.

Water-based paint is simpler to apply (although advances in the technology of making oil-based paint have improved it out of all recognition) and has no smell. It is easy to wipe up spills or smears, and it has an attractive flat, matt or silk finish. It also has the advantage in ordinary applications of drying very quickly. Water-based paint is usually used for walls and ceilings.

Oil-based paint, if used at the recommended manufacturer's consistency, is more difficult to apply and get smooth, and any spills have to be wiped up quickly with white spirit. It is available in different compositions: matt, eggshell, satin and gloss, depending on the degree of reflectivity required. Because of the oil content, it can take quite a long time to dry, forcing you to wait between applying coats. It is mainly used for furniture and woodwork.

Although oil-based paints have traditionally been used for special paint effects, the recent improvements in water-based paints, with extended drying time, have allowed them to be used as an alternative.

ESTIMATING PAINT QUANTITIES

Determine the square footage of the project you are undertaking by taking the vertical and horizontal measurements of each wall and multiplying them together. Then add the total for the four walls. For example, the walls of a room measuring $3.1 \times 2.5 \times 2.5$ m/$10 \times 8 \times 8$ ft high would be 7.75 sq m/80 sq ft plus 7.75 sq m/80 sq ft plus 5 sq m/64 sq ft plus 5 sq m/64 sq ft – a total of 25.5 sq m/288 sq ft. Check the label on the can of paint to see how much square footage it will cover if you use it undiluted. If you thin the paint by one-third for example, it will cover a third as much again.

APPLYING THE BASE COAT

Any painted surface will need a base coat. Professional painters, for sound reasons, have an order of work to prevent dribbles spoiling their work. They start with the ceiling, then do the walls, then window and door frames, then the doors themselves, then the cornices and finally the skirtings.

If you are using a roller, you will need to go around any edges with a brush first, as the roller cannot get into corners or close to any proud edge. Mask any areas that might get paint inadvertently brushed on to them with tape.

Apply the paint in a criss-cross pattern, never directly up and down, and try to finish the area with a nearly dry brush. Work from the top of the wall down, and do not stop until you have finished a complete area or you may get a tidemark where you stop, particularly if you are using quick-drying paints.

APPLYING THE GLAZE

Almost all paint effects are achieved using a glaze which is worked into with a brush, rag or comb to produce the required finish. The consistency and composition of the glaze depends on the technique you are using but in all cases the glaze has to be wet when you work on it.

There is now a wide variety of ready-made, water-based acrylic glazes that you can use for broken paint effects, but they do dry out much more quickly than the old oil-based glazes. You can get round this problem to some extent by working with a partner, one of you applying the glaze while the other stipples, sponges, drags it or whatever. The advantage, however, is that these glazes are less smelly and the brushes can be cleaned with water. If you do not varnish the surfaces afterwards, they are also easier to redecorate.

This antique bath may well have been bought in this condition, but the aged appearance is one that you can copy easily on modern fittings and furnishings, by painting a brown base coat with a lighter colour over it, and then rubbing it with wax and fine-grade steel wool to achieve a patchy show through which imitates authentic wear and tear (see page 111).

Varnishing

M ANY DECORATIVE paint techniques are not particularly wear- or waterproof, and they are normally finished off with a coat or two of varnish in any area which is subjected to damp or a lot of wear. Not only does this protect the finish from chipping, rubbing off or moisture damage, but it can also add a sheen to the surface. A varnished surface can be wiped clean if needed. Varnish can also be used to change the finish of the surface from matt to mid-sheen or gloss.

There is a range of different varnishes on the market but they fall into three principal categories: oil-based, alcohol-based or the more modern acrylic-based types. Oil-based varnishes have now largely been superseded by acrylic-based varnishes which dry more quickly and do not yellow in the same way that oil-based ones do.

Wood-graining – here a walnut-type finish – has been used to give this studio room the appearance of panelled walls, helped by the imitation of the wooden supporting struts. The finished effect has been varnished to imitate the polished patina of real wood.

One drawback of any varnished surface, however, is that it does not provide a good key for the paint to adhere to in redecoration. Varnished surfaces will need to be sanded down and primed before being repainted. Bear this in mind because it will lengthen the preparation time for any future redecoration you may wish to do.

The type of varnish you choose depends on the materials you have used for the paint effects. Acrylic-based varnishes are normally only used over acrylic- and water-based paints and are thinned down with water; polyurethane- and oil-based varnishes can be used over either water- or oil-based paint and are thinned with white spirit or turpentine.

Varnishing must be done in a dust-free environment, otherwise tiny particles of fluff and dust will adhere to the sticky surface, marring the finish. To get a good result, use the varnish as thinly as possible, applying a second coat if needed when the first coat is dry. For a better finish, the first coat can be lightly sanded with fine-grade sandpaper before the second coat is applied.

Any paint residue adhering to the brush will spoil the finish so it pays to keep separate brushes for varnishing. To clean such brushes, soak them in white spirit (for oil-based varnishes), methylated spirits (for acrylic-based varnishes) or water (for water-based varnishes). Then wash out and dry thoroughly in the usual way.

TYPES OF VARNISH

Oil varnish Can be used over both oil- and water-based paints. Is thinned with white spirit. Takes a long time to dry and yellows. Will therefore change the appearance of light colours quite noticeably. Tough-wearing and waterproof.

Polyurethane varnish Can be used over oil- and water-based paints and is thinned with white spirit or paint thinner. Yellows less than oil varnish, but will do so a little. Dries quicker than oil varnish. Tough-wearing and waterproof.

Shellac Alcohol-based varnish, used in French polishing. Can be thinned with methylated spirits. Dries rapidly, but yellows and is very brittle. Can be used on paper card to make it tough enough for stencils (see page 99).

Acrylic varnish Can be used only over water-based paints and is thinned with water. Dries fast and yellows only slightly.

Wax Not really a varnish, but is used to give a sheen to painted finishes, particularly in ageing and distressing (see pages 111–113). Can be removed easily and reapplied. Is not water or wearproof. You cannot apply varnish over it.

SURFACES FOR PAINTING

Paint is far more versatile than most people imagine and it allows a marvellous range of expression in design terms, from the individual patterns of stencilling, block printing and découpage at its most elaborate to rich textural effects such as imitation wood-grains and marbles. Walls, floors, doors, wooden furniture, fireplaces, lampshades, screens and even fabrics can all provide the base for decorated paint finishes, of which many (see pages 63–79) are aimed at imitating more expensive materials.

Some of the best effects are produced by combining a variety of paint techniques – stencilling and distressing an old wooden chest, for example, or using one finish for the dado area of a wall, another for the chair rail itself and yet another for the area between the dado and the picture rail or ceiling.

Once the surface has been primed (see page 49) to take the paint, almost any type of paint finish can be used on any surface. However, some of the decorative paint techniques are more difficult to work than others, and are best kept to smaller areas.

CEILINGS

These are tortuous to paint so do not opt for some elaborate finish unless you are a masochist! In a bathroom, you should either use a waterproof paint or coat an emulsion paint with varnish, otherwise the damp atmosphere will probably cause it to peel or crack. Remember that dark colours reduce the height of a ceiling. If there is no cornice, consider incorporating one. You can buy polystyrene cornices which you simply stick on, prime and paint.

WALLS

Bathroom walls too must be finished with some kind of waterproof medium if oil-based paint is not used. As bathrooms are generally fairly small, you can opt for more time-consuming techniques, such as imitation marble or stone. In bedrooms, the softer effects of sponging, stippling, ragging or colour-washing are particularly appropriate, especially if combined with an area of pattern in the form of stencilling or block printing.

Remember that you can change the proportions of the room by dividing up the wall space, with a chair rail and/or a picture rail and treating the intervening spaces with different paint effects – perhaps imitation wood-graining for the dado and frottage for the area between the chair rail and the picture rail. If you do this, be careful with your choice of colours. It usually pays to go for toning effects or gentle contrasts. Too sharp a colour division will

create too strong an impression and dominate the room uncomfortably. Pay attention to colour saturation (see page 13) when choosing colour combinations in these circumstances.

Panelled effects can be remarkably successful in bedrooms, particularly if you want to try out an elaborate technique but do not want to expend the time and energy to carry it out over the whole room.

DOORS AND CUPBOARDS

These can be treated in a range of ways. If you have cheap blockboard doors, you might consider using wood-grain effects (see page 85) or imitation marquetry (see page 88). Dragging and combing are both also attractive finishes for doors and cupboards. Marbling is a good alternative for bathroom fittings and cupboards. Remember that the furniture does not have to be made

This bedroom demonstrates how paint effects can be used in different ways on different surfaces. The headboard of the bed has been marbled, as has the plant container, while the walls behind have been spattered in yellow ochre on a paler yellow ground. Note the way that different types of marble have been imitated for the headboard and the container.

of wood. You can paint melamine just as satisfactorily provided you prime it properly first, and you could transform a range of rather impersonal, brilliant white fitted bedroom cupboards into something altogether more individual. Don't forget the handles, however – you may be advised to change any little gilt ones for something more in keeping with the new effect.

FREE-STANDING FURNITURE

Individual items of furniture can be treated in a variety of ways, depending on their character and the style of the room. Newish items can be successfully aged to fit in with a more general period style; small tables can have stencilled images applied, and they can be given a variety of textural finishes. Try not to give the furniture a finish that is totally inappropriate for its style – you will not like the final result. The easiest pieces to paint are those with fairly simple shapes, and without elaborate carving or beading. Dull-looking plain but battered items frequently seen standing forlornly on pavements outside junk shops are ideal material for the amateur paint decorator, and perfect to practise on.

FIREPLACES

Imitation wood, stone or marble effects come into their own here, and can transform a rather drab-looking fireplace into something that gives the room a real focal point.

CAUTION

Many of the products used in painting are toxic in some way, and you need to be very careful about inhaling the fumes or getting the product on your skin (or indeed in your eyes). Read the manufacturer's instructions carefully; wear a mask, gloves and/or goggles if recommended, and if using an unusual product for the first time, dab a tiny bit on your skin to see if you get an allergic reaction. If you do, either do not use it or take special precautions.

Pay particular attention to the manufacturer's warnings on ventilation; otherwise you could well suffer from unpleasant side effects – headaches and nausea, for example – if you are exposed to the fumes for too long or in too concentrated a form.

Some artists' colours and pigments are also toxic – particularly those with a chrome or cadmium base – so again take care and pay attention to what you are using and doing.

In this close-up of the bath featured on page 39 you can see how successfully the water-lily design imitates the way that the flowers naturally float on the water surface.

BROKEN PAINT TECHNIQUES

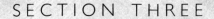

THIS SECTION covers the principal techniques used to create attractively mottled paint finishes. In their most basic terms, these are paint effects created by simply moving thinned-down paint in the form of a glaze around on a previously painted base coat.

Although relatively simple in terms of the ingredients used, a professional-looking finish does take practice to achieve, although less professional-looking effects have a charm of their own. The skill comes in mixing suitable colours, judging the consistency of the glaze, and working quickly and evenly, applying the same pressure throughout.

Sponging

THE ART of successful sponging lies in creating a gently mottled effect using at least two colours that are fairly close to each other in tone. It is, in my opinion, more attractive than a completely plain stretch of painted wall, and it has the advantage that, if the plasterwork is less than perfect, it helps to hide any flaws as the mottling prevents the light from highlighting any bumps.

SPONGING OFF

This technique consists of applying a thin coat of glaze over a base coat, and then removing some of it with a natural sponge to achieve a mottled finish. It creates a more subtle and attractive finish than using the sponge to paint on to the wall.

Since most walls require more than one application of paint, the time taken to apply the base coat and then sponge another colour on to it is only marginally longer than normal painting. The sponged-on coat is normally used thinner than the base coat – you can use emulsion paint thinned with a little water or an acrylic paint also thinned with water.

The only tool you require is a natural sea sponge – its irregularities help to give a pleasantly varied look to the mottled surface which a mass-produced foam sponge fails to achieve. You will also need a roller tray in which to pour the sponging medium for ease of use.

1 Over a previously painted base coat of vinyl silk or eggshell (white in this case) brush a thin oil-based scumble glaze (roughly the same consistency as single cream, and tinted with Indian red in this case). Brush it out using criss-cross brush strokes over panels about 60 cm/2 ft wide. You do not have to produce a particularly even finish since this glaze coat is worked into while it is still wet. The aim is to work fairly quickly.

2 Using a natural sponge dampened with a little white spirit, start to dab the sponge lightly over the wet glaze. Try to keep a rhythmic movement going, with a slight twist to the wrist, to create an even-looking mark. The more heavily you press, the more glaze you remove, the lighter the finish and the less distinct the mark you leave. The choice is yours.

3 This shows the 'wet edge' – the area of brushed glaze that you leave unsponged at the edge of the panel you have just completed. It is important to leave this wet edge, so that you can feather the glaze for the next panel into it, thereby ensuring you do not create a 'tide mark' where the panels join.

It is a good idea to keep a couple of damp cloths handy to wipe off any areas of sponging which do not blend successfully as you work.

The main secret of sponging is to work lightly and quickly. Don't overload the sponge or you will just get a splodge of paint rather than the dappled effect you are trying to create.

As with all paint finishes, try it out first, either on a small area of the wall that you can paint over afterwards, or on sheets of card.

If you use contrasting colours, remember that light over dark colours give a ghost-like effect, and dark over light will be more translucent. The marks, however, will show up much more noticeably, and if you are a novice, it would be a good idea to practise with more subtle colour combinations where any unevenness or errors are less likely to show up.

More advanced sponging techniques include sponging on more than one colour. It pays to apply the darkest colour first, and you can get very good results by simply lightening the tone of the same colour with each application, by adding more and more white to it.

Sponging off is a variation of this technique, in which you apply a fairly runny glaze over the base coat with a brush and then use a damp sponge to remove the paint in dabbing motions. Unless the area is small, you really need two people for this technique if you are using a water-based glaze as it all has to be done fairly fast before the glaze dries. One person applies the glaze, the other removes it with the sponge. If you try doing it on your own, it all becomes rather frenzied unless you are ambidextrous and can apply the glaze with one hand, and dab it off with the other! You need to make sure the sponge is cleaned regularly, as if it becomes clogged, you lose the effect you are hoping to achieve and you end up with a messy splodge instead.

If you use an oil-based glaze, the drying takes longer so you have more time to carry out the

4 When you apply the glaze for the next panel, make sure that you work into the wet edge of the previous panel with the brush to remove any demarcation line.

5 Here a second deeper shade is being sponged on over the first coat to give a deeper, richer effect.

6 The finished area completely sponged. You will find that it takes practice to be able to repeat an even-looking mark but keeping the sponging off movement light, regular and rhythmic, and cleaning the sponge at frequent intervals, will help. The same effect can be achieved using an acrylic base coat and acrylic glaze, if you prefer, but they do dry much more quickly than oil-based paint. If the finish is for a bathroom, varnish it when it is dry.

technique, but a water-based glaze gives a flatter finish.

If you want to be really subtle, you can use both sponging off and on in combination, using first the sponging-off technique, allowing the surface to dry and then sponging on a second coat.

Once you get used to the idea, you will probably start to develop your own techniques and favourite

The walls in this bathroom have been sponged in two shades of sea-green over a white base coat and then varnished to give a smooth, glossy waterproof finish.

recipes. It is not an exact science and much depends on the look you want to achieve and whether you find, by accident probably, a form of marking that you think looks attractive.

RAGGING

AGGING ON and ragging off are exactly the same techniques in principle as sponging on and off, but you use a rag instead of a sponge. The effect is more varied and is probably rather easier, since inconsistencies in application techniques show up less. You normally use an oil-based glaze for the ragging on or ragging off coat.

The rags themselves are normally ordinary cotton cloths, but you can achieve different results using different types of fabric. A cloth that is hard and not very porous, like cotton, will achieve a more defined mark. Softer cloth, like cheesecloth or muslin, will produce, unsurprisingly, a softer result that looks a bit more like sponging.

Rag-rolling, as the name implies, is another version of ragging, only using a rolled, rather than a bunched, rag. The effect is slightly softer and less bitty-looking, but also slightly more laborious, and you have to pay more attention to the marks you are making with the rolled rag. Like most techniques, the more you do it, the better you get at it. A bathroom would be a good place for a first attempt, since the area to be covered is usually fairly small. The only unfortunate aspect is that when you are lying in the bath, you have little else to focus on except the paint technique on the wall in front of you, which may make you rather critical of your efforts!

RAGGING OFF

1 As with sponging, the first step in ragging off is to apply a coat of thin oil-based scumble glaze with a brush in 60 cm/2 ft wide panels. In this case a mixture of Prussian blue and terre vert artists' oils has been mixed with white to tint the glaze coat, which is the consistency of single cream. Remember that a very little artists' oil colour will go a surprisingly long way. Add it with caution.

2 Tear old white sheeting or similar fairly coarse cotton into a number of thin strips, and scrunch up one of these to make a loosely bunched up rag and start to remove the glaze by dabbing the bunched rag lightly across the glaze. Leave a wet edge (see page 64) around the area you are ragging to feather in the next panel.

3 Continue to apply the glaze to the next panel, working into the wet edge of the previous one to ensure no demarcation line is left between the panels.

4 Carry on ragging off the wet area of glaze in panels as before until the entire area is completed. As soon as the rag becomes paint-sodden, throw it away and start again with a piece of clean cloth. When you have completed the entire area, leave it to dry completely.

5 To add a second colour, brush a thin coat of oil-based glaze tinted in a second colour that is fairly close in tone and hue to the first, and work, as before, in smallish panels. In this case, slightly more Prussian blue has been added to the previous glaze colour.

6 With a clean rag, start to remove the glaze as before, using rhythmic dabbing motions and replacing the rag as necessary to ensure the marks remain fairly distinct.

7 The finished ragged effect, using a second colour. As you can see, the effect is richer, deeper and subtler with two coats rather than one. It is worth taking the time and trouble to apply a second colour to achieve just this richness of effect. Again, if you want to create a waterproof finish, varnish it once it is completely dry.

RAGGING VARIATIONS

There are a number of variations on ragging, which are worked in exactly the same way but using different media to create the marks in the glaze. Frottage is the name given to the technique that uses newspaper, and there is another variation in which polythene bags are scrumpled up to create the marks. In both cases, you need to renew the paper or bags being used frequently, so ensure you have a good supply before you start.

Newspaper makes a softer mark in the paint than rags, and polythene bags a rather sharper-looking one. Your choice depends on the kind of finish you want to achieve.

These very roughly colour-washed and ragged walls have been executed in a very thin wash of bright pink over white, giving a suitably loose, rough effect that works well in this simple cottage bedroom, the pink walls and yellow door picking out the colours in the antique quilt.

FROTTAGE

If you want a deliberately rough-textured finish that looks like aged plaster, you can opt for frottage – a technique in which newspaper is used to create irregular marks in the paint.

This is a good technique for a novice because it is not the aim to produce a perfect finish, and frottage therefore covers a multitude of sins. You can work it perfectly easily with a water-based paint that has been roughly applied with a brush, on to which you then apply newspaper, pressing it gently into the wet paint and then removing it to create the pattern.

The skill comes in getting the paint to the right consistency so that you can create an attractive, but irregular, pattern.

You can use an oil-based paint, but be aware that the paper will absorb quite a lot of it.

The finished effect of frottage. To create a less marked effect, wash over it with a thin coat of watered-down emulsion or apply a second coat and frottage it as described below.

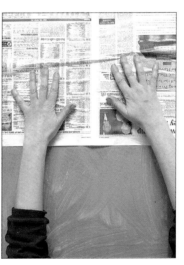

1 Unlike the previous paint effects, frottage is done with silk emulsion paint that has been thinned to the consistency of single cream with water. Paint the base coat (white in this case) and allow to dry. Then brush over the watered-down emulsion coat (here tinted with yellow ochre and Indian red acrylics) in a criss-cross, fairly rough and ready fashion.

2 While this coat is wet, flatten a sheet of newspaper on to the paint and press down well. Then pull the paper off after a few seconds. Repeat with fresh sheets of paper over the surface being worked.

3 This is the effect with the paper removed. As you remove the paper, you take some of the paint with it. The aim is to produce an unevenly marked finish, rather like rough plaster. It is ideally suited to cottage walls.

CHEESECLOTHING

Contrary to what you might expect, the coarser weave of cheesecloth creates a finer, more delicate mark than that produced with the standard cotton rag used in ragging. Although the technique is executed in much the same way, using the cloth to partially remove the previously applied oil or acrylic glaze, the result is rather like a cross between ragging and stippling. Unlike stippling, cheeseclothing does not need to be particularly perfect, making it a simpler alternative for a novice than stippling, which, to look good, has to be worked with very even pressure.

To get a smooth, even texture when cheeseclothing, you do need to fold the cheesecloth carefully into a well-rounded even pad, in which the ends of the cloth are tucked, so that you do not get any sharp lines or angled marks when you start to remove the glaze.

Once the pad starts to absorb too much paint, it will not produce the appropriate textured surface. Re-fold the cloth to reveal a clean part, and when that is used up, use a new piece of cloth. You will need to have a good supply of strips of cloth for a large wall.

As with all paint effects, you can use more than one colour for the final result (see Colour-washing, page 72, for technique).

The paint used for this effect can be either an oil-based glaze applied over an eggshell or vinyl silk base, or an acrylic water-based glaze over an acrylic or vinyl silk base.

If you wish, you can combine it with another paint technique to 'soften' the effect. For example, you could rag off the first colour and then cheesecloth the second one to give a rather more blurred final pattern. However, make sure that both coats are either oil-based or water-based.

1 Over a base coat of vinyl silk (for water-based glaze) or eggshell (for oil-based glaze), apply the glaze coat in rough criss-cross brush strokes.

2 Tear the cheesecloth into largish rectangles (about 45 cm/18 inches square) and fold into a neat pad, tucking the ends in so that the working area is completely smooth. Start to dab off the glaze with the pad in light, even movements. A fine almost stippled-looking surface will result. Keep a wet edge (as described in Sponging, page 64).

3 Work in panels about 60 cm/2 ft wide and complete these, before moving on to the next panel, keeping the wet edge open. The photograph, above, shows the finished effect.

COLOUR-WASHING

THIS PRODUCES a wonderfully soft, subtle-coloured surface that is far more interesting to look at than an area of flat paint, and yet less marked than the sponging or ragging effects shown on pages 64 and 67.

Colour-washing has three steps: one to apply the base coat, a second to apply the glaze, and a third to wipe it partly off. The secret of success is to use a very thin glaze coat which can be either oil- or water-based. The former dries more slowly, giving you more time to work, and the final effect is slightly shinier and deeper-looking. You can work with a sponge or with a very soft brush to remove the glaze, depending on which you find easiest to use.

Since the glaze for this technique is a lot runnier than other glazes, it is messier to work with. Make sure that all surfaces not being painted are covered. Do not get anxious if the first coat is very patchy-looking. The second coat, as you can see from the photographs opposite, makes a vast improvement.

Experiment with colours to suit your particular scheme. When using two colours, pick a second colour that is close in tone and hue to the first one used. Blue–grey, blue–green, yellow–apricot or Indian red–ochre are all colours that work well together over a plain white base coat.

If you wish, you can also colour-wash furniture, described in more detail on pages 89–90.

1 If you are using an oil-based glaze, paint the base coat in an eggshell finish. If you are using a water-based glaze, use a vinyl silk base coat. When the base coat is completely dry, brush on the first glaze coat (in this case tinted with yellow ochre) in a rough criss-cross fashion. This glaze should be much runnier than that used for other decorative effects – watery rather than creamy in consistency.

2 Apply the glaze in panels about 60 cm/2 ft wide, keeping the wet edge open (as shown in Sponging on page 64). At this stage, it does not matter if the brush strokes look patchy and uneven.

3 While this glaze coat is still wet, use a soft rag (cheesecloth is ideal) rolled up in a pad to remove some of the glaze and even out the marks. Use a light, brushing rubbing movement to create a soft, blurred effect.

4 This is the final stage of the first coat of glaze, brushed out so that the effect is light and translucent. It will not look particularly even, but that is part of the virtue of the effect, which is meant to resemble distempered walls.

5 Wait until the first coat of glaze is completely dry before applying a second one. Then apply a second coat of glaze in a toning colour (here a mixture of burnt sienna and Indian red) in a rough criss-cross fashion, working in the same size panels as previously.

6 As in step 3 of the first coat, start to remove some of this layer of glaze with a soft, bunched-up rag to even the colour out and remove the brush marks.

7 When this second coat has dried, the effect is much more attractive as there is a variation in tone and depth of colour that makes the unevenness look much more natural. If you are using colour-washing in a bathroom, varnish it when dry with matt, polyurethane varnish.

Colour-washing can be used for furniture as well as walls, as this small chest of drawers demonstrates. It has been colour-washed in yellow and Indian red to produce an almost terracotta-coloured finish. It is better to use oil-based paints and glazes on furniture to prevent the grain rising and the wood warping.

SPATTERING

THIS TECHNIQUE involves directing the paint at the wall in such a way as to break up the surface into tiny dots or blobs. These blobs can vary from coloured flecks of paint to watermarks produced by flicking a thinner, such as turpentine, on to a painted surface. Whichever one you opt for, be aware that the process is likely to cover you – and everything else in the room – in paint unless you take avoiding action! In spattering, you can use an acrylic-based glaze over a silk emulsion finish.

You can, if you wish, hire a spray gun, which may take you a while to get used to before you can produce even results, but the traditional methods involve striking a loaded brush of paint with another object or using birch twigs.

The effects can be eye-catching and exciting, particularly if more than one colour is spattered over the base coat. The technique known as spattering off, in which turpentine is flicked over a stippled oil glaze, is particularly attractive with its myriad of tiny watermark-like dots. However, you are unlikely to be able to master it successfully on a vertical surface, because of dribbles and runs.

You can spatter paint over other paint finishes, such as sponging, if you like.

 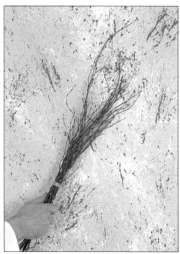 

1 Mask off adjacent areas with newspaper and cover all surfaces. Wear an overall and goggles! Over a beige base coat (emulsion is fine for this technique), and using a bunch of birch twigs tied with a rubber band at the base, start to flick a coat of white emulsion over the base coat. Dip the end of the twigs in the paint, and use a flicking motion of the wrist.

2 Allow the first coat to dry. For the second coat of Indian red emulsion, use a clean bunch of birch twigs and repeat the technique in the previous step.

3 For the third coat, repeat step 2 using cobalt blue paint. Try to spatter the paint so that the colours are distributed fairly evenly across the surface.

DRAGGING, STIPPLING AND COMBING

DRAGGING, STIPPLING and combing are all variations, in a sense, of sponging and ragging. The main difference is that the patterns are rather more visible, creating a slightly textured effect to the surface. The degree of pattern and texture depends on the kind of tools used, and the choice is a wide one. Precisely because the patterns are more noticeable, it is harder to keep them even over very large surfaces, and this kind of texturing is mostly best done on smaller areas. The more noticeable the pattern, the more skill and confidence are required. It is a once-and-for-all job – you cannot go over it, as you can sponging or ragging, to correct any mistakes.

An oil-based base coat and oil-based glaze are normally used as these give the best results and definition, but acrylic-based paints can also be used, although you will need to work more quickly.

Dragging is an excellent finish for cupboards or doors if you use an oil-based glaze, as it gives a good sheen but the colour is more diffused than with a plain colour, and looks very elegant.

1 Over a base coat of eggshell (white in this case), apply a coat of oil-based glaze, tinted in this case with burnt Sienna. Unlike the previous decorative paint effect techniques, in dragging this first glaze coat is applied in an up-and-down direction only.

2 Using the same brush, working into the wet glaze, go over the surface smoothing out the glaze, working in a vertical up-and-down movement to create an even finish.

DRAGGING

This is done by dragging a soft, long-bristled brush (known as a flogging brush) vertically through the glaze (also applied in vertical lines) to produce fine lines in the surface. This is far easier to do if one person applies the glaze and the other drags it off.

STIPPLING

Stippling, in which the paint surface is broken up evenly and lightly by a fine-bristled brush, creates an attractive finish which is very lightly textured. Professional decorators use a very expensive stippling brush but you can succeed with an ordinary scrubbing brush, although the paint dots will be larger and less even.

This technique can only be done with an oil-based base coat and oil-based glaze, because it

This door panel has been dragged in terracotta on a white ground, to pick up the colour used for the wall, creating a softly blended effect.

3 Using the flogging brush, go over the same area in even vertical movements to create fine vertical lines. Wipe any surplus glaze off the brush between strokes.

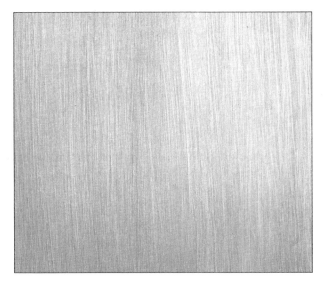

4 The finished effect should look even and smooth. On larger areas where you may have to stop the dragging movement before a whole vertical line is completed, make sure you do so at different points on each panel so that there is no waterline mark running across the wall.

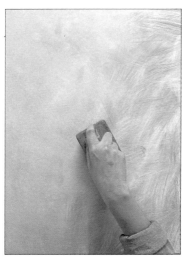

1 Over a base coat of eggshell (white in this case) apply a coat of oil-based glaze, slightly thinner than the normal consistency of single cream. Here the scumble glaze has been tinted with Indian red artists' oils. Brush it roughly in criss-cross fashion in panels about 60 cm/2 ft wide.

2 With a stippling brush (a wide brush with short, stiff bristles), go over the wet glaze by striking it with the stippling brush in short firm movements. It is very tiring to do so, do not over-reach your limits on your first attempts.

3 Go over the stippled finish with a rolled-up cotton rag to soften it off. Do not roll the rag tightly into a sausage shape but use it loosely bunched. Throw it away once it starts to absorb too much paint and start again with a fresh rag.

needs to stay wet enough for you to break up the recently painted surface with the brush.

It is quite tiring to work, and you will find it better if you just use your wrist to apply the stippling brush to the glaze, fairly lightly and quickly. Again it will be easier for you if you can work with a partner, one of you applying the glaze while the other stipples it.

You tend to get the best results by using a slightly paler base coat than the glaze, so that the former glows through the latter.

If you want to give character and depth to architectural features, or perhaps to a raised paper like anaglypta or lincrusta, you can employ this technique. The aim is to get a deeper, darker layer of paint in the crevices and grooves of any feature by stippling the paint on first, and then wiping off the areas that are raised.

You need an oil-based glaze, ideally in a darker shade of the base coat.

4 The finished effect makes an attractive blend of the lightly mottled finish produced by the stippling brush with the rather more distinct marks made by the rolled rag.

COMBING

This is really an exaggerated form of dragging with a more distinct patterning. Instead of the fine vertical lines created by a stiff bristle brush used in dragging, a variety of differently toothed combs can be used. These can either be bought specially or you can make them yourself by cutting notches in pieces of cardboard or plastic to the width and density required.

With combing, the pattern is not necessarily vertical. You can try different patterns, including basketweave (a mixture of horizontal and vertical stripes in alternating squares) or moiré, curved, or criss-crossed patterns.

The base coat is applied in the usual way (see page 54) and a glaze applied over it. This is stippled or cheeseclothed lightly to break it up before being combed through.

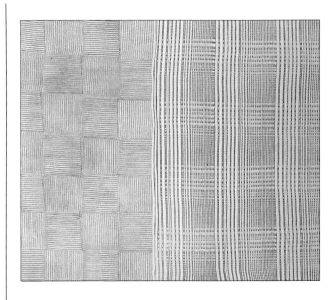

Two different combing patterns, produced using combs that have different tooth configurations. The basket weave pattern on the left used a finer-toothed comb. The tartan pattern on the right was done with a coarser-toothed comb.

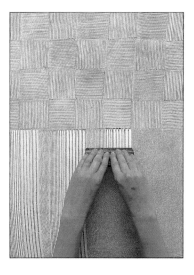

1 Apply a rough coat of oil-based glaze (tinted here with terre vert and Prussian blue) over a base coat of eggshell (white in this case) and remove some of the glaze by going over it lightly with a rolled-up pad of cheesecloth (see Cheeseclothing page 71).

2 Using a fine-toothed comb, press well into the wet glaze using both hands on the shank of the comb, and create a basket weave pattern by taking the marks at right angles to each other in similarly sized squares. If you want to make a very perfect finish, you will have to measure these out. Done by eye, as here, they look pleasantly informal.

3 To create a more obvious mark, use a wider-toothed comb. In this, the first step of a tartan effect, simply drag the comb through the glaze in vertical lines. To create the tartan, go over these combed lines at right angles leaving regular spaces between each set of combed lines.

TEXTURE AND PATTERN

THIS SECTION covers a range of more advanced or unusual effects and the different surfaces on which they may be executed, including wood and fabric. There is no limit to what can be created – all depends on the imagination and ability of the decorator. The most difficult effects are those involving freehand painting. To do this successfully, in an ambitious way, involves some degree of artistic training, although surprisingly satisfying results can be achieved by copying other work.

This section also includes a number of 'cheat' techniques to create surface effects that mirror others – for example, painted effects that mimic actual wood grain, and marbling, in which the eye is literally tricked into believing that something is what it is not.

Fabric painting, which is touched on briefly, could be the subject of a book in its own right, and indeed sometimes is. However, many of the techniques shown in this book can be successfully translated for use on fabric.

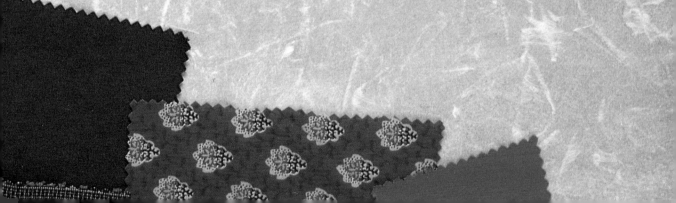

TRICKS OF ILLUSION

ONE OF the great virtues of paint effects is that they can be used to imitate, extremely successfully, materials that cost a great deal more. Among the tricks of illusion in the paint decorator's repertoire are imitation marble and imitation woods, such as mahogany, walnut or pine, as well as imitation stone effects.

It has to be said, however, that these are not beginners' techniques. Only those with the confidence that comes from experience can produce really successful results, although you do not necessarily have to practise on large areas.

Considerable artistic ability is shown in this skilful example of trompe-l'oeil. *The choice of colours adds to the illusion by emphasizing the perspective.*

Marble is one of the most traditional materials for a bathroom but it is extremely expensive. You can create an aura of sumptuous luxury by imitating it or fine woods, such as maple or satinwood that were popular in furniture design in the 1930s.

A more elaborate form of imitation, *trompe-l'oeil* (which means, literally, tricking the eye) demands even greater skill and should not really be attempted by anyone who does not have a reasonably strong artistic bent, unless you are just aiming for very simple effects, and have at least some facility with a paintbrush.

IMITATION WOOD EFFECTS

Among the simpler imitation wood effects that you can create with paint are *bois clair*, pine and mahogany. The aim is to reproduce, as clearly as you can, the actual knots and grain marks of the natural woods.

If you are trying to match an existing piece of furniture, then your job is made easier because you can study its graining pattern and try to copy it.

Usually, the base coat is slightly lighter in colour than the glaze that is applied over it, with which you create the graining pattern. Depending on the type of wood, it may help if the base is one which has already been sponged or stippled, to produce a mottled finish before the fine graining lines are made with a brush.

To get an authentic finish takes practice, time and patience, but quite acceptable results can be achieved by relative novices provided they work systematically. Do not attempt very large areas while learning these techniques, and practise first on a piece of board until you obtain a successful combination of colours and marks.

BOIS CLAIR

ONE OF the easiest wood finish techniques for a relative novice is *bois clair* (pale wood). It gives the impression of fine polished woods like maple or satinwood that have relatively little grain in them. The famous Biedermeier furniture, designed in Germany in the 1930s, made much use of these pale golden-yellow smooth woods. You could use the technique to create a bathroom in this period style, by painting the bath surround in a *bois clair* finish. Make sure that the rest of the bathroom is in keeping with the style, by using pale, neutral colours with touches of black, and plain white bathroom fittings.

Any imitation wood finish in the bathroom is best given a coat or two of varnish to make it waterproof. You can use either an acrylic-based glaze or an oil-based one, as you prefer. An acrylic-based glaze will definitely need varnishing afterwards, and the oil-based one would be better varnished.

For this technique you need a special, long, soft-bristled brush (a decorator's flogging brush gives good results) or you could use steel wool to produce a similar effect. The aim is to get the paint to form a light, uneven texture.

To create the *bois clair* finish, apply a base coat of white or pale beige eggshell, and when this is dry, apply a coat of yellow-tinted oil glaze (using a combination of yellow ochre and raw sienna artists' oil colours). Work into this while it is still wet with a long-bristled, soft brush. If you push the brush down into the glaze, rather than dragging it along, you will create the knotty look of maple or satinwood.

1 Prepare a base coat in warm beige and allow to dry. Then mix a glaze using yellow ochre and burnt sienna (or similar light yellow-toned browns) and apply it over the base coat, fairly roughly.

2 Work into the wet glaze with a flogging brush to create a streaked and mottled effect. Allow this coat to dry.

3 Then apply a second coat of glaze in a slightly darker brown, and work into it in the same way. For bathrooms, varnish the finished effect, when completely dry, with matt polyurethane varnish.

Grained Wood

T O IMITATE the natural, random pattern of wood grains is an art in itself. If you wish, you can copy nature precisely and repeat the exact graining patterns of the different woods. It may have escaped your notice, but these are all completely different. Pine, oak, mahogany and walnut, to name a few of the familiar woods used for furniture, all have a markedly different graining pattern and colour.

However, you do not have to be so precise and you can create perfectly satisfactory, generally

Opposite   Combined with the marble surfaces in this bathroom, the decorative wood finishes create a very luxurious, rich effect. A pale bois clair finish has been applied to the panelled walls and cabinets, with a darker glaze to simulate the knot marks. The brass light fittings are most appropriate for such a décor.

appealing, wood-grained finishes for doors, skirting boards or dados, for example, that simply have a generally grained pattern. The technique is very similar to dragging, but the bristles in the brush are softer, making a less clear-cut mark in the painted surface.

Any eggshell-finished surface can be wood-grained. It is particularly useful as a technique if, for example, you want to make modern doors less conspicuous in a room that contains antique furniture.

Prepare the surface and paint two base coats of eggshell finish in the appropriate shade of brown for the purpose. Then prepare an oil-based glaze tinted with burnt umber artists' oils. The graining effect is achieved by a mixture of stippling or sponging and dragging.

1 Over a base coat of eggshell (in this case white) apply a fairly dry oil-based glaze (without too much white spirit or turpentine) and brush it out well over the surface in vertical, as opposed to criss-cross, brush movements to resemble the grain lines of wood.

2 With a piece of cheesecloth bunched into a pad, go over the wet glaze and rub it down to soften the brush marks, but keeping the slightly vertically lined effect.

3 With a purpose-made graining rocker, drag it down through the wet glaze with both hands, as evenly as you can. Where you stop the dragging motion, you will create an oval knot-like effect in the graining lines. Try to keep these knots at irregularly spaced intervals, to resemble natural wood.

4 Go over the grained wood with a soft, long-bristled flogging brush to soften and blur the grain marks.

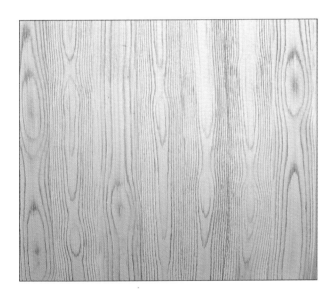

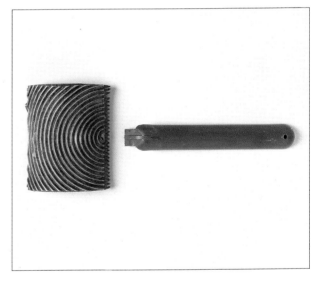

5 The finished effect. Note how the knot marks have been randomly spaced to create the natural appearance of real wood. You can, if you wish, create a more realistic effect using natural wood colours, but pale greens and blues look attractive, resembling the effect you get when using wood stains on real wood.

6 The specially devised rocker for decorative graining effects. The handle screws into the rocker, but when you use the tool, press down with both hands on either side of the handle on the back of the rocker itself for greater control.

Good use has been made of decorative paint effects in glowing golds and browns: the tallboy has inset wood-grained panels, the walls have been frottaged and even the cushions on the easy chair have been stencilled.

If you wish, pre-mixed coloured scumble glazes and base colours appropriate for different types of wood can be bought at specialist decorating shops.

DECORATIVE GRAINING

This technique aims to simulate the natural grain of wood, but without specifically copying the grain and knot marks of any particular wood type, such as oak, pine or elm. As a consequence, it is much easier to execute satisfactorily, since the overall effect you are aiming for is simply one that looks good in its own right. It is far harder to copy a specific wood, since not only do you need to get the grain marks to look fairly realistic, you need to match the colours as well.

Decorative graining can be achieved using a variety of techniques, but one of the forms that works well is shown on pages 85–86. Having applied a base coat, you then need to apply the oil-based glaze, which is cheeseclothed and then dragged through with a long-bristled brush to produce delicate vertical lines. While this is still wet, take a wide-toothed comb, or a purpose-made rubber rocker, like the one shown left, and draw it in gently down through the glaze. Where you stop, you will create a surprisingly lifelike grain and knot mark. Make sure these appear at irregularly spaced intervals.

It is a technique that definitely requires practice to master, so try it out first on a piece of card or board until you are satisfied with the effect.

Staining Wood

OOD CAN be treated in a variety of ways using different paint effect techniques, but it is worth remembering that you can also use wood-stains – transparent liquids that colour the wood while allowing the grain to show through – if you prefer. Wood-stains can be used very successfully on all types of wood, to create wonderfully delicate colour-washed effects as well as much deeper, richer colours. They are either spirit-, alcohol- or water-based. The modern range of colour-stains are usually water-based and therefore easier to use. They come in a variety of colours rather than simply those that imitate the natural colours of different woods.

They can be applied direct to bare, unprimed wood but on wood that has been previously stripped, you should prime the wood first with a coat of thinned-down acrylic varnish to make the wood less absorbent and to ensure that the stain is applied evenly.

You can either opt for an overall effect, using the stain to colour the piece of furniture, floor or door in its entirety or you can use several colours of stains for a more decorative finish.

To create a marquetry-type effect, draw out a very simple geometric design, such as star-shape, on the surface in pencil and then cut lightly around the pencil lines with a sharp scalpel to prevent the stain seeping and running. Paint in the areas of the design using different colours of stain, as required. Alcohol-based stains are useful for this kind of design as they dry quickly.

You can coat the finished design with varnish or simply wax it with good quality beeswax polish, depending on the amount of wear.

You can use either purpose-made wood stains or a thin coat of emulsion as a colour-wash to produce this watery effect in which the texture and grain of the wood show through, as they do with these colourful palettes.

COLOUR-WASHING AND LIMING WOOD

ALTHOUGH SOME professional decorators may raise their eyebrows at the thought of using water-based paint on wood, it is perfectly possible to do so provided you use one of the modern vinyl-based emulsion paints, and do not make the wood too wet.

You will need to remove any trace of previous varnish or wax; and ensure that any wood that has been chemically stripped down is first neutralized with a solution of vinegar and water (one part vinegar to 20 parts water).

One of the advantages of colour-washing wood is that it provides a range of colours while allowing the natural beauty of the wood to shine through. It is the ideal choice for wood that has a naturally raised grain, such as chestnut, pine or oak.

For floors, and any areas that need to have a hard-wearing surface, the finished effect should be sealed. Sand the wood lightly after colour-washing, apply a sanding sealer and then varnish it.

Alternatively, lime the wood after colour-washing it.

1 Prepare the wood first, removing all wax or varnish. Then brush on a thin coat of woodwash colour (you can buy this purpose-made or you can use a vinyl emulsion but make sure the latter is not too wet and that the effect is fairly dark – Prussian blue emulsion was used here). Allow this coat to dry completely. It does not matter if it looks patchy.

2 Using liming wax and a very fine-grade steel wool, apply the wax liberally, rubbing it both with the grain and across the grain to make sure that it is well absorbed into the wood.

3 Allow the liming wax to dry for about 20 minutes, and then go over it with clear beeswax and steel wool, which will remove the top layer of liming wax while giving the wood a sheen. Throw away the steel wool when it gets clogged with liming wax and start afresh with a new piece.

4 Allow this coat to dry off for about 10 minutes and then buff it up with a soft cloth. The white liming wax should adhere to the grain marks giving the wood an attractively bleached appearance.

5 The finished effect. As you can see the final colour is considerably paler and more bleached out than the first coat of woodwash. It is best to experiment with a small area initially to ensure that the final effect has the right colour density, as the wax will considerably bleach the original colour.

LIMING

Although not strictly a paint technique, liming is often used in conjunction with colour-washing to change the character of wooden furniture, and for floors or panelling. It was used originally to protect wood from attacks by woodworm, as the slaked lime used in the paste was a powerful deterrent. Unfortunately, it also did considerable damage to those applying the paste! However, today's liming wax is a much more innocuous mixture of white pigment and wax, which produces the same visually attractive result without any of the inherent dangers.

Liming gives a bleached appearance to the wood, as the liming paste adheres to the wood in the crannies between the grain lines. It is a wonderful means of transforming heavy, rather plain dark oak furniture or those highly varnished pieces from the 1940s into something infinitely more attractive. Oak, ash and elm, which all have a strong grain pattern, are ideal candidates for liming. Pine can also be limed, but needs to be brushed with a wire brush to make the grain lines stand out more.

You can buy liming wax at any good paint supplier, but, if you prefer, you can make your own out of beeswax polish and white pigment (see box below). Before you can apply the liming wax, you will need to strip any existing varnish or paint off the piece of furniture, using one of the specially formulated paint strippers now on the market. You may then need to go over the surface of the wood with a copper brush to bring up the grain as much as possible.

If you wish, you can also colour-wash the wood first using a coat of watered-down emulsion paint. Watered-down blues, greens and greys make particularly good base coats for the liming process, creating a Scandinavian-style finish.

If you lime a piece of furniture with decorative moulding, the effect is enhanced as the liming wax tends to adhere to the grooves, and you can then buff up the prominent pieces of moulding to give an aged appearance to it.

Liming has transformed this rather plain cabinet into an elegant piece of furniture (new handles would have helped!). Look out for similar items in second-hand furniture shops. You will have to strip the varnish off first, which can be laborious although there are now many good proprietary stripping products.

If you want to varnish the finished surface, you will need to use a water-based liming paste, made from a mixture of white pigment, water and a little glue, rather than using liming wax, over which you cannot apply varnish.

RECIPE FOR LIMING WAX

Heat some clear beeswax furniture polish in a double-saucepan until it melts. (Do not put in a saucepan over a direct flame – it would probably catch fire, and do not heat the wax over too fierce a heat as it may create poisonous fumes.) Add some Titanium white pigment in the ratio two parts polish to one part pigment and stir well. Pour into a pot and allow to cool and set.

IMITATION MARBLE

THERE ARE many different types of marble, depending on the area where it is quarried, with different base colours and veining patterns. Among the oldest known sources of marble, used by Michelangelo for his sculptures, is Carrara in Italy.

With paint effects, the aim is to create an authentic-looking base colour and veining pattern, not to reproduce the marble exactly. Normally you will need an eggshell base coat to give the underlying colour, over which a toning oil-based glaze is applied which is worked on in one direction with either a brush, rag, sponge or plastic bag to give the underlying pattern, depending on

the particular kind of marble you are aiming to copy. When this coat is completed, any additional veining is painted in. You will need a special brush made of very soft hair, called a badger softener or blending brush. It is not cheap but you cannot achieve the smooth sheen of marble without it.

Marbling can also be done using water-based paints and glazes, which have the advantage of drying much faster than oil-based paints and glazes but you will not be able to produce the sheen and translucency that oil-based paints give, and you will have to work quickly because of the shorter drying time. Much depends on how realistic you want the finished effect to be. Any water-based

1 Over a base of beige eggeshell, and working in smallish panels about 60 cm/2 ft square, start to apply the first coat of slightly darker oil-based glaze in diagonal, but not crossing, lines (using an artists' brush) to resemble the veins of real marble.

2 While the glaze is still wet, start to blur the edges of the marks using a softening brush. You can use a sponge in the other hand to dab the colour to break it up and mottle it slightly.

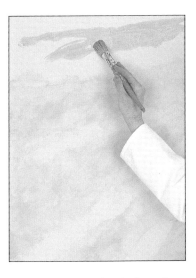

3 Allow this coat to dry. Apply another coat of glaze in either the same colour or a lighter or darker tone, depending on the final effect being aimed for, and repeat the procedure outlined in step 2.

paint effect used for a bathroom must be varnished afterwards to make it waterproof, otherwise it will crack and peel.

You can create imitation marble effects on all kinds of surfaces, but they look particularly effective painted directly on to a cast-iron bath tub, for example. Floors, dados, fireplace surrounds and lampstands are all suitable areas too.

The lighter coloured grey and white Carrara marble or the golden Siena marbles are easier to copy than the dark green or black ones, because the veining pattern is less obvious and therefore any mistakes are less noticeable.

This attractively marbled dado has the variation in colour density and veining mark that makes all the difference when marbling. It requires time and patience to produce this quality of effect but the finished result is well worth the effort involved.

4 Allow this coat to dry completely. You can now draw in finer lines with an artists' brush in a different coloured glaze to make more distinctive marks.

5 With an artists' brush, repeat the earlier procedures at random points across the surface, making sure the grain lines run in the same direction. Soften and blur as before with a sponge and a softener.

6 The finished effect. For a bathroom this finish must be varnished to make it waterproof.

STONE EFFECTS

I T MIGHT well appeal to you to create a baronial-style bathroom, for example, with imitation stone walls. Imitating stone is not particularly difficult, especially if you choose a fairly small area such as a bathroom. However, it will make your work easier if the areas you are tackling are clear of bathroom fittings, so consider adding some kind of dado or tiling above any fittings and use this technique for clear areas of walling.

There are as many different types of stone as there are types of marble, but you do not necessarily have to aim for perfect verisimilitude. The aim is to create a pleasingly realistic stone-like effect. It helps to make it look more authentic if you try to reproduce the texture as well as the colour.

CREATING A SANDSTONE EFFECT

You will need to paint the wall first with a coat of white emulsion, unless the wall is already white, in which case just wash it down. The base coat does not need to be applied particularly carefully because the base colour for the sandstone effect is a pale beige eggshell that is stippled over the top.

You can go for a more realistic effect by painting in the mortar lines between the 'stones' or you can simply give a stone-like appearance to the wall.

To create the sandstone effect, first mark the stone shapes (using a spirit-level and plumb-line) in pencil on the white emulsion base, remembering to draw the blocks in the same way that bricks are laid, with the joints staggered. Then stipple on a thick coat of pale beige emulsion paint roughly, painting almost up to the drawn pencil lines. If you paint each stone separately, you will get minor variations in texture that will give it a more realistic effect. When this coat is dry, brush on a transparent oil glaze coloured with a little burnt umber artists' oil paint, allow this to dry for a few minutes and then wipe it off with a cloth.

After the glaze has dried, brush on some diluted white eggshell paint roughly. When this has dried, you can sand the surface down to reveal the pale beige emulsion underneath, creating a suitably rough, uneven texture to the finished surface. Finally, draw in the mortar joints, freehand, in pale grey emulsion, using a paintbrush. If you are using this effect in a bathroom, then varnish the finished surface to make sure it is waterproof.

These imitation stone walls have been created using colour-washing techniques in off-white and grey-beige, with grisaille (shadowing) techniques used to give the impression of panelling.

CREATING STRIPES AND CHECKS

WITH THE aid of some low-tack masking tape (and a spirit-level or plumb-line for getting the stripes horizontal or vertical as required) you can create some interesting geometrical patterns of stripes and checks.

You can either go for clean-cut stripes, possibly to create an imitation chair rail on a wall for example, in which the colour is carefully masked

MAKING ROLLER STRIPES

This technique is done freehand using a smaller than average roller (about 15 cm/6 inches wide). A more exact stripe could be created with a plumb-line and masking tape. Here, the stripes were painted over painted woodchip paper.

using the tape or you can paint stripes using a roller, overlapping the edges slightly. When making stripes of this kind, make sure that the paint is not too runny. For painting stripes on fabric, see page 122.

Stripes can be used to break up large flat expanses of wall, to alter the dimensions of a room. Dividing the wall up horizontally in this way will succeed in making a high-ceilinged room look smaller and more intimate. Vertical stripes will make a large room look smaller.

You can use whatever type of paint effect you want for making the stripes. At its simplest it can

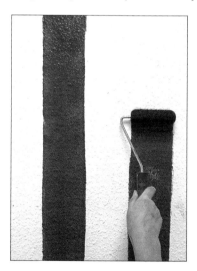

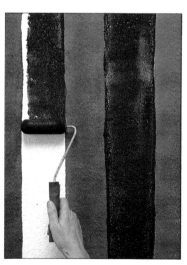

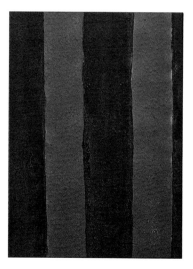

1 Over a plain emulsion base coat, paint the stripes with the roller, leaving a roller's width between each stripe. Allow this coat to dry. If you wish, you can stop at this point.

2 To create contrasting stripes, paint in the spaces between the roller stripes with another colour. Allow the colours to overlap slightly, and make sure any unfilled areas are covered with paint.

3 The finished effect. If you want a blurred finish, you can paint the second stripe while the first is still wet, allowing the edges to run and bleed. This technique works effectively, for example, on lampshades, or on roller blinds, as the fabric encourages the paint to bleed of its own accord.

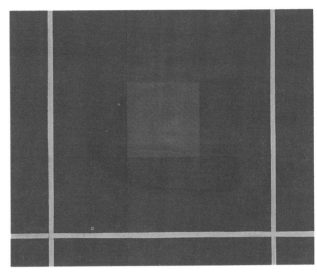

This neat tartan effect has been created using masking tape to section off the squares of colour over a base coat of bright red. The whole design was drawn out first using a set square and a pencil. A fine pale grey stripe was added as the finishing touch.

A highly colourful, jazzy version of freehand painted stripes, taking the inspiration for the colour scheme from the bedcover. The door panels and bedboards have been given a similar colour treatment, but in spots.

provide a simple colour contrast to provide, say, a border between the wall and the ceiling or to outline a door or window frame. Various decorative paint effects can be used for the stripes, depending on their width. To create a softer appearance, you can colour-wash the wall afterwards using an almost transparent glaze, which will simply remove any harshness from the pattern. Alternatively, use only subtle colour contrasts for the stripes – mauve and grey, pale pink and white or soft ochre and cream.

If you are painting stripes on wood, it may be advisable to score the wood very lightly with a scalpel along the edges of the masking tape to make a barrier for the paint.

Plaid effects can be created using masking tape, together with several tones of the same colour. The base coat will need to be a lighter shade of the predominant colour over which darker shades of the same colour are applied in turn, masking off the areas as appropriate.

Soft plaid effects can be achieved by not masking off the colours, and deliberately allowing the edges to bleed into each other. The appropriate consistency for the paint is important, so that it does run too freely but is thin enough for the edges to blend. Practise first on a board, propped up vertically if you are going to paint on a vertical surface, and thin the paint down gradually until you get the required consistency for blending without the paint dripping.

This soft plaid effect works particularly well on fabric where the paint has a tendency to blur and blend if the fabric has not been sized first. It would look attractive on cushions and lampshades (see page 119), for example.

STENCILLING

STENCILLING IS one of the most versatile decorative paint techniques. The size, shape and nature of the patterns used are entirely a personal choice, as indeed are the paint finishes used to create them. You can go for isolated, individual stencilled images, or repeating patterns to make borders. In days gone by, before wallpaper was manufactured, whole rooms were stencilled to look like wallpaper. Nowadays, if you want such overall patterning, it makes more sense to use paper patterns or block prints, but if what you want is an individualistic, personal touch, then stencilling is the answer.

You can do as much or as little of the design and making up of the stencil as you wish. You can buy, nowadays, whole ranges of stencil patterns from a variety of suppliers, but it is more fun, and not particularly difficult, to make your own templates for the pattern.

HOW STENCILLING WORKS

You can stencil almost any surface, from walls and doors, to lampshades and blinds, and you can use almost any colouring medium that you want. The template for the stencil is lightly secured to the

MAKING YOUR OWN STENCIL

1 Find a design you like (perhaps, as here, you want to recreate a design from a piece of fabric) and enlarge or reduce it on a photocopier (if necessary). Lay the copy on a flat surface and put a sheet of tracing paper over it. Draw in the outline in soft pencil.

2 Go over the design carefully with a very soft pencil (3B) to bring the image out on the reverse side so that it makes a transfer.

surface in question with masking tape, and the paint, ink or dye, applied over it carefully, so that the cut-out pattern of the stencil is transferred to the surface below.

A reverse form of stencilling can also be used whereby you cut out the shapes required, stick them to the surface securely but lightly, and paint over the whole area. On removing the stencils carefully, these areas will be unpainted.

On large areas, it makes more sense simply to paint the stencil patterns in. On small objects, such as lampshades or trays, reverse stencilling can be just as effective.

In the case of lampshades, it is particularly striking if the lamp is painted, for example, a warm golden brown, the chosen stencilled shapes stuck on the shade, and then an overall coat of a much richer rust-coloured paint applied. When the stencils are removed, and the light switched on, the translucent golden brown coat will show up the stencilled patterns beautifully.

MAKING YOUR OWN TEMPLATES

Almost any flat item that will successfully mask the surface below can be used as a stencil, from masking tape to leaves or paper doilies. However, cut stencils are normally made from either oiled card or from acetate. You can prime your own card quite easily or you can buy it ready-made. It is easier to work with card than acetate because it does not slip as much, but it is inclined to tear more easily. The advantage of acetate is that you can see through it, making any pattern in which the stencils have to be lined up much easier to use.

The first step in making your stencil is to trace the design you wish to use on to the oiled card. If the design is too small or too large for your purposes, the easiest way of enlarging or reducing it is to use a photocopier with this facility. Once you have traced the design, you have to transfer it to the stencil card or acetate. You can do this much

3 Turn the stencil over to the right side, fix it in position with masking tape on the stencil card (making sure you have left a good-sized border around the design) and rub the design with some kind of hard implement (the end of a pencil, for example) so that the design transfers on to the stencil card.

4 Cut the stencil out with a very sharp scalpel blade. If it is to be used for a border, you will need to cut registration notches (small slits or holes) in the card surrounding the stencil so that you can line the patterns up together.

more easily on acetate, because it is transparent. Simply place the tracing under the acetate and draw over the outline with a felt-tipped pen. With card, you will have to use carbon paper to transfer the shape.

When cutting out the stencil, use a very sharp scalpel blade and always remember to leave a generous margin of card or acetate around the image so that you avoid accidentally splashing paint on the surface below.

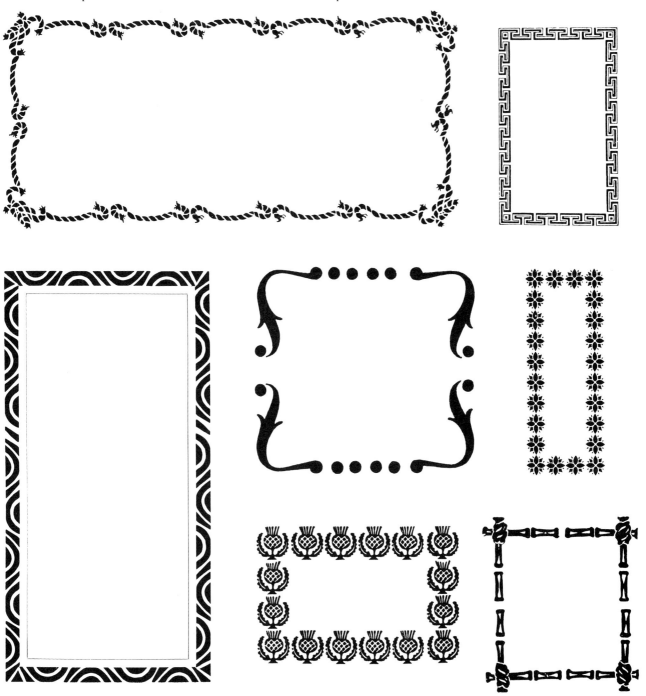

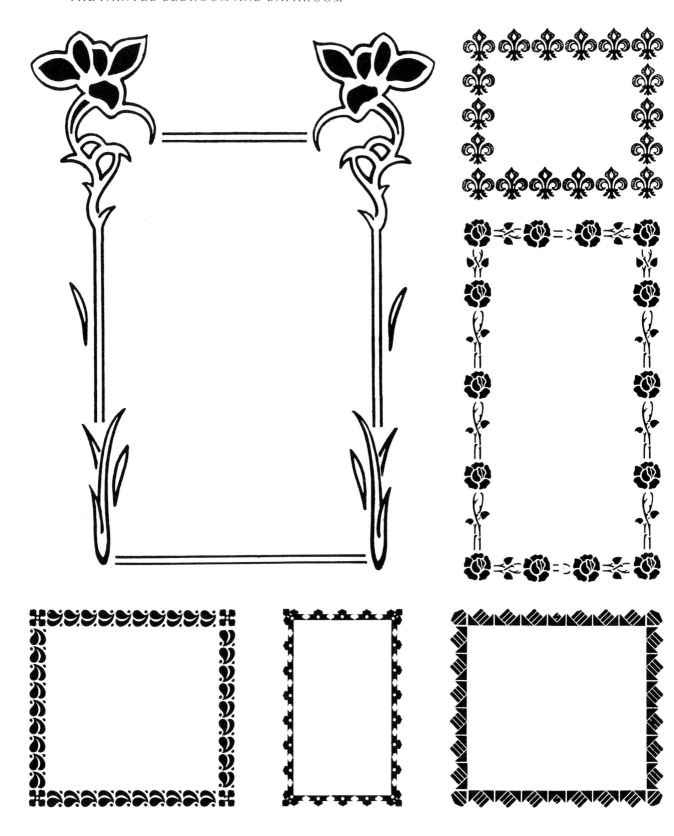

MAKING STENCIL CARD

Although you can buy stencil card quite easily from any art supply shop, you can also make your own if you prefer. Use thick cartridge paper or manila card, and brush both sides of the paper with linseed oil. Leave it to dry for several days.

When you store the stencils, lay sheets of paper between them to prevent them tearing. Any tears and rips in the card can be mended with masking tape.

Two stencil patterns – a Greek key pattern at cornice height and a rolled rope pattern at dado height and around some of the pictures – have been applied over these sponged and colour-washed walls. Stencil colours should be kept soft and muted – they look particularly good when applied over surfaces with decorative paint effects, as this also blurs and softens the final effect.

PAINTS AND EQUIPMENT

The kind of paint to use for the stencil will depend on the surface being stencilled. Emulsion paint works fine on walls, for example, and can either be applied with a soft brush or a sponge, or sprayed on (provided you remember to mask the area off properly so that the paint is not inadvertently sprayed on the walls as well).

Proprietary stencil paint is also often used, as are stencil crayons which you mix with water and then apply with a stencil brush. Car-spray paint can also be used, but this requires a rather specialized technique (see page 105).

The main point to ensure is that the paint is neither too runny nor applied too thickly, although you also need to make sure it covers the entire area of the pattern to be stencilled to achieve a proper outline. If you build up the colour slowly, you will create a more attractive, three-dimensional quality, and you can also make multi-coloured stencils, using a different pattern for each colour.

Decide on the area for the design, and how it is to appear. Then, using a pencil, mark the area lightly on the surface to be stencilled. If, for example, you are stencilling a row of shells as a border, make a series of small pencil dots on the surface to be stencilled to indicate the position of the stencils. You can tape the stencil in position, or if you are confident, simply hold it in one hand, using the other to apply the paint.

COLOUR AND TEXTURE

The most successful results in stencilling seem to be those where the pattern is soft and muted, blending gently with the underlying surface. If you decide after you have stencilled a border that the effect is too bright, you could always colour-wash the whole wall afterwards, painting over the stencil as well, to tone it down a little.

Stencils also look particularly good applied over distressed paint surfaces – on sponged or ragged walls, for example – as these tend to soften the outlines of the design.

IDEAS FOR PATTERNS

The choice of patterns is almost limitless and depends on your own taste. There are a number of excellent sources for designs. Several publishers (see page 125) produce books showing traditional designs, which you can use for inspiration. Museum shops are often a rich source of pattern books, prints and postcards which will yield attractive designs, as are many of the ethnic shops with prints and postcards of different tribal and folk designs.

Fabric around the house can also be used as a source of ideas. A curtain pattern could have one motif copied from it, and repeated on a mirror, tiles or lampshade. Be wary of stencilling too many surfaces; it can start to look rather tasteless.

Alcoves, door panels, drawers, mirror frames, shutter panels, bedposts and fireplaces, as well as architraves to doors and windows, are all suitable places for stencils; the fabrics used for firescreens, lampshades, blinds, bedheads and bed-drapes, curtain tie-backs, curtain borders and pelmets are suitable too (see page 116). In the bathroom, shower curtains can be stencilled, as can ceramic tiles, cisterns, bath surrounds and cupboard doors.

STENCILLING A FLOOR

Stencilling can be carried out on a range of surfaces, including floors. Some of the most successful designs mimic oriental carpets, with an all-over pattern which has been carefully worked out to create a *trompe-l'oeil* floor rug, painted on bleached wooden floors.

A less time-consuming, but equally attractive idea, is to stencil a border around the perimeter of the floor, and this could be a worthwhile option, perhaps, in a room that has a large rug or square of carpet in the centre.

In the step photographs (see right) a stencil border is applied to a cork-tiled floor. If you want to stencil a floor that has been varnished, you will have to sand it down before painting it.

Muted paint colours that blend well with the natural wood of the floor are the most successful.

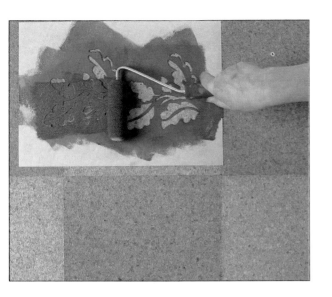

1 Line up the stencil and use masking tape if necessary to hold it in position. Apply the paint to the stencil with either a stencil brush or a roller. Here, a PVA/emulsion paint mixture has been used with a roller but proprietary stencil paint can also be used, with a stencil brush if you prefer. The paint must be thick enough not to seep under the bridges of the stencil.

2 Repeat the stencil pattern along the border, lining it up as required. Create a narrow border, if desired, using masking tape and the edge of the roller to apply the paint, or you can use a narrow brush.

3 A finer, inner stripe has been added to the border to give it more definition, using the same technique outlined in step 2.

4 Varnish with several coats of proprietary floor varnish to seal well. Failure to seal the floor well enough, will result in the stencil wearing patchily.

5 The finished effect. It could just as easily be applied to floorboards or hardboard as these cork tiles, but in either case the floor must be prepared properly first and must be clean and grease-free.

The impact should come from the interest that the pattern creates, rather than from the colour. Muted blues, greens, Indian reds and greys work well, particularly in conjunction with colour-washed or limed floors.

Quick-drying water-based paint is the easiest to handle, but remember that it will need varnishing to prevent the pattern being worn away with use – normally at least two or three coats are required to give a durable finish.

You can also stencil a cork floor to give a 'lift' to it. Make sure that any polish or varnish is removed before applying the paint.

Below   This wood floor has been stencilled and then limed and waxed, creating a soft, subtle finish. Avoid using bright colours for floor stencils.

STENCILLING ON CERAMICS

Retiling a bathroom is a chore, apart from being expensive. If the tiles you have are acceptable, but boring, then it may well be worthwhile considering stencilling a pattern or a border on to them, to add a bit of life to the overall decoration.

You may find it easiest to opt for a random pattern rather than a rigidly applied overall pattern, simply stencilling the odd tile here and there, or, perhaps, adding a border to the area just above the bath or basin.

Car-spray paint is ideal for stencilling in a bathroom because it is very durable and you do not have to seal the finish. Like all spray paint, it is messy to use and you need to mask off the surrounding areas extremely carefully if they are not to become marked.

You get a better effect with car-spray paint if you diffuse it – in other words spray it on to a piece of card held at an angle to the stencil card (as shown below). This will ensure only a fine mist falls on the stencilled area, with a much more attractive result.

2 Holding the car-spray paint about 15 cm/6 inches from the stencil, direct the spray sideways on to another piece of card held at an angle so that it diffuses on to the cut-out stencilled area. This makes the sprayed image more subtle and reduces the risk of blobs of paint spoiling it. If you want a multi-coloured effect, spray again with a second or even third colour when the previous coat or coats are dry.

1 Plain ceramic tiles can be given a touch of individuality by stencilling them using car-spray paint. Attach the stencil to the tiled area with masking tape. Here a small stencilled motif has been attached to a larger piece of card to provide an adequate shield to prevent the paint from spraying inadvertently on to surrounding tiles.

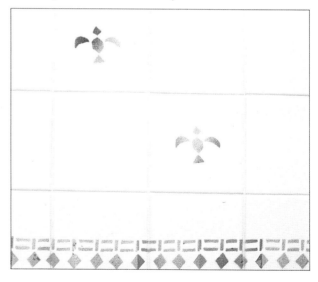

3 The finished effect, complete with stencilled border. Car-spray paint is extremely hard wearing but it is also fairly toxic. Work in a well-ventilated space, use a mask (and rubber gloves if your skin is sensitive) when handling it, or follow the manufacturer's instructions as appropriate.

Always practise first on a piece of board to ensure that the strength of the final colour (or colours if you use more than one) is as you intend it to be. Even a slight variation in the angle of the card will affect the result.

These attractively stencilled ceramic tiles have been decorated in gold and blue, probably with a spray diffuser. The wall behind has been crackle glazed (see page 114 for techniques).

BLOCK PRINTING

BEFORE THE mechanization that took place during the nineteenth century, printed patterns on walls or fabric were made using stencils or block prints. For the blocks themselves, all manner of objects can be used from vegetables and corks to carefully carved wood.

The medium for the colour can be ink or paint. Even children's paints will suffice, although you will have to varnish them afterwards so as to make them washproof.

The secret of getting an even impression is to coat the block with an adequate amount of paint, and then to apply firm but even pressure to the block, without movement, to print it. It is essential to make a trial run on a piece of board, painted with the same medium that you are planning to use as the base coat, to check that the consistency of the paint is suitable. If it is too runny, the paint will dribble down the wall, if you are printing on a vertical surface, or form an unattractive ridge around the design on a horizontal one. Too little paint, and the image will not print clearly enough.

Some unevenness in the printing is part of the charm of this technique – do not aim for perfection. It would be a waste of time if it looked like manufactured printing! The aim is to get a pleasantly hand-crafted effect, without any blobs, runs or splodges.

1 This very simple block printing technique uses a square of synthetic sponge on a plain white emulsion surface. Pour the emulsion paint (here a pale ochre has been used) for the block printing into a roller tray and press the loaded sponge on to a sheet of card to check the density of the image. Then apply the sponge to the surface pressing firmly and squarely.

2 Make the chequerboard design by lining up the corners of each square. Clean the sponge as necessary to prevent it becoming blocked with paint. The aim is to produce a slightly broken image. Irregularities are part of the attraction.

3 Once the printed design is dry, go over it with a coat of thinned-down emulsion wash in white to soften and blur the outline of the print. The finished effect is exactly the same as step 2, but slightly paler in colour.

Craft shops often sell attractive small wooden blocks, but if you prefer, you can make your own. Wood carving demands too much skill for most amateurs, but it is perfectly possible to carve a good block out of polystyrene or synthetic fine sponge. Equally, you can make blocks from firm-textured

The walls have been rubber-stamped and a stencilled border added at cornice height. To get this soft effect, give the walls a coat of thin colour-wash after stamping.

vegetables, such as potatoes. Let the potato dry out for a day before using it for a block, so that the juice does not mingle with the paint.

DECOUPAGE

DECOUPAGE HAS the same roots as collage, and it is a form of poor man's art, since the images you use are normally those created by other people. In fact the Venetians called it just that – *arte povera*. It is a collection of cut-out images applied to form an overall picture, which is then applied to an artefact, such as a screen, firescreen, lampshade, mirror frame or tray.

It can only be called a decorative paint technique if you stretch the term a little, because it does not always necessitate using paint, although you can equally well use cut-out black-and-white images which you then colour in. In order to get a really smooth finish, the finally stuck-down image has to be varnished many times. It is, therefore, time-consuming to carry out, but can also be extremely enjoyable.

The image can be applied to any painted or varnished surface, whether fabric, metal or wood.

Magazines are probably the best source for images but you need to be careful that the show-through that occurs on printing does not become exaggerated with the wetness of the glue or varnish. Greetings cards, old seed packets and wrapping paper are other good sources.

Although the background to the découpage was traditionally plain, there is nothing to stop you applying pattern to pattern.

1 Choose a suitable image and photocopy it, if necessary, to achieve the number of images for the project. You could have one central image on, say, a chest of drawers, or you can use découpage to decorate a wall with randomly placed images, as here. Start to cut away the background from the image neatly with a sharp pair of scissors.

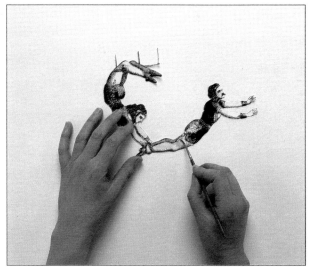

2 Using an artist's brush and gouache, acrylic or poster paints, colour the image if you wish, either entirely or partly. These Victorian-style acrobats are simply being tinted like an old-fashioned photograph.

When cutting out the images for the découpage, be careful to use only the sharpest scissors or a scalpel knife so that you can cut them neatly and accurately.

The glueing must be carefully done, and all the edges absolutely secure. Use a paper glue where you can wipe away any excess cleanly and easily.

If you are using photocopies as sources for images for découpage, they can be coloured in by hand to assume some of the delicacy of Victorian cut-outs. Alternatively, certain publishers, such as Dover, produce books of facsimiles of Victorian découpage designs, which you can simply cut out and use, like a child's pattern book.

When colouring a photocopy, take care not to make the paper too wet. It helps to stretch the paper on to a piece of board using masking tape to hold it in position, to prevent it from buckling as you work. Settle for a limited palette of colours – perhaps two or three – using them simply to tint the photocopy rather than colour it completely.

Once the paint is dry, the image can be cut out in the usual way.

3 Position the images on a clean dry surface and paste down using paper glue. Make sure that the edges are really firmly stuck down. Wipe a damp sponge over afterwards to smooth the glue towards the edges of the images and to remove any surplus glue.

4 When the glue has dried, apply a coat of matt, polyurethane varnish and allow this to dry. You will probably need to build up several coats of varnish to achieve a completely smooth finish.

5 The finished effect. If you wish to give the image an aged or antiqued look, you can go over it with a dark wax polish and then buff it up. This looks particularly good when applied to old wooden furniture.

AGEING AND DISTRESSING

IT MAY sound like a contradiction to suggest that surfaces that are newly decorated are then deliberately made to look old, but certain styles depend on the patina of age for their appeal. And the appeal lies primarily in the fact that the colour looks 'faded' rather than new.

Half the appeal of many antiques is their 'aged' appearance, adding value frequently to the piece. My sister, when living in Greece, wanted to buy an old coffee pot as a present. The owner of the little shop she went to only had brand-new, shiny copper ones for sale. She asked him if he had any antique ones. 'Come back tomorrow,' he said, 'and it will be antique.' She did, and he had turned her pot into a perfect replica of an old one, probably by kicking it a few times and rolling it in dirt!

If you like the rather shabby, lived in and homely look of a house that has seen some action, and equally dislike the brassiness that sometimes goes with newly painted finishes, then ageing is your answer. It has the estimable virtue that it will not show up the marks, knocks and stains as easily as a plain, flat-painted surface, and will therefore last far longer. It does, however, require skill if it is not to look simply old and uncared for. If you do opt for this antiqued look on modern furniture, any handles should be changed to something appropriate.

If, for example, you were going to put a new pine dado in a room that had comfortable, but fairly old-looking furniture, then ageing the wood would help to make the dado look as though it belonged to the room.

1 Paint the surface with dark brown emulsion paint (one of the new proprietary mixtures of PVA and emulsion is ideal) to provide a base coat. Allow this to dry. Then apply a contrasting second coat of paint, quite roughly, over the top with a brush, leaving some show-through of the first coat.

2 Apply a coat of dark beeswax polish with fine-grade steel wool and rub it well into the painted surface, taking off some of the paint and scoring it a little in places.

The paint colours that work best are either the soft blues, greys and sage greens that you tend to see on sun-bleached paintwork in the Mediterranean region, or the more vivid peeling colours of Mexican or Caribbean plaster work. One of my favourite colours is the rich pinky terracotta plaster seen on many houses on the Mediterranean shores of northern Italy. The sun has faded the colour in places, so that it is a myriad different tones of the same hue.

The aim is to reproduce precisely that kind of weather-worn appeal. To make this work successfully, you need to distress the places where wear would most naturally occur – on any raised areas, for example. False cracks and holes can also be incorporated, using darker paint. To do it well takes time and patience, with several layers of paint in softly varying shades of the same colour.

When you are stencilling any surface, a degree of antiquing helps to make it blend well with the surface underneath.

STENCILLING AND DISTRESSING

If you wish to stencil a piece of furniture and give it an antique appearance, apply the stencil in the usual way (see page 103). When this has completely dried, mix together some clear furniture wax and apply over the piece of furniture, including the stencilled area, rubbing it in gently with finest-grade steel wool. Leave the wax to dry for about 15 minutes and then polish the surface with a soft cloth. Using fine-grade sandpaper, rub parts of the surface away gently before adding a second coat of the wax polish and treating it in the same way.

You can use this technique on panelling, doors or wooden furniture.

Opposite This small cupboard has been very attractively antiqued using three different colours, to provide a contrast between the frame and the door panels. The aim when antiquing furniture is to give it just this natural, uneven appearance. If the patchy colour is too regular, it looks false.

3 Allow to dry off for about 15 minutes and then buff it up with a soft cloth to give the surface a good sheen.

4 The finished effect. If you have painted your base coat of brown over an original light coat of paint, you need to take care that you do not scrape so much of the second and third coats away that the white shows through. In this instance, you may find you need to give it more than one base coat of brown paint to prevent this happening.

AGEING ARCHITECTURAL FEATURES

One of the best ways to lend character to a room, especially in a house that has little in the way of interesting architectural features, is to add your own mouldings and then 'age' them using decorative paint techniques. Dado rails, picture rails and plaster ceiling mouldings can all successfully be given this treatment.

Using a satin-finish oil-based paint, apply the base colour to the moulding. Make up a glaze comprised of raw umber and burnt umber artists' colours in the following proportions: six parts of oil glaze to one part of thinner, and follow the stippling instructions on page 78. The parts of the moulding that stand out in relief are then wiped off.

A richer, more three-dimensional effect, can be achieved using more than one colour of glaze, ideally only very slightly different in tone and colour from the first one. When you have applied and wiped off the first coat of glaze, apply the second colour in the same way.

A rather more authentically aged appearance can be given by allowing the stippled colour to overlap the surface below, wiping it off with a rag and then stippling it lightly again with a dry brush.

CRACKLING

THIS IS one of the simpler techniques but it is also extremely effective. The surface of old oil paintings naturally cracks into fine hair-like cracks in the fullness of time, and restorers painstakingly remove this varnish and apply a clear new coat, in part at least because the old varnish dulls the colours of the original.

The technique of crackle glazing has been used by decorators to age pieces of furniture deliberately (and probably by forgers to age paintings deliberately!) and it has its own distinctive appeal.

The method shown here consists of sandwiching a layer of crackle medium (available at most specialist paint stores) between two layers of emulsion paint. The medium reacts with the paint, causing it to crack into a crazy effect of small broken lines.

Another technique consists of applying two different kinds of varnishes, one oil-based and one water-based, which react in a similar way to the paint, by cracking into hairlines.

Crackling can be used on a variety of surfaces, but it is ideally suited to picture and mirror frames, to door panels or lamp bases, for example. A coat of dark wax over the finished crackled look helps to give it that authentically aged appearance. The wax adheres to the fine cracks, naturally darkening them.

One of the best colour combinations to use for crackling is a light cream or beige over a dark brown, blue or browny red, so that the darker colour shows through the fine hairline cracks.

1 Over a coat of dry emulsion paint as a base, apply a thin coat of crackle medium (available from specialist paint stores) as evenly as possible, and allow it to dry. The thinner this coat, the finer the eventual cracks will be.

2 When it is very nearly dry, paint on a second coat of emulsion paint in a contrasting colour. Make sure that you apply the paint in complete single strokes – do not overpaint a brush stroke of the medium will start to lift the paint off. You will start to see the crackling effect almost immediately.

3 When this coat has dried you can either varnish it or you can age it by applying dark beeswax to the surface with fine-grade steel wool, rubbing it well into the cracks.

4 When this has dried a little, remove the surplus wax with a soft cloth.

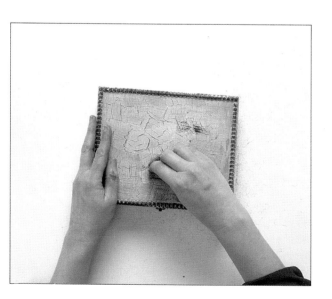

5 If necessary, rub it down a little more with fine-grade steel wool to produce more show-through of the first colour if you wish.

6 The finished effect, showing both the fine hairline cracks and the first coat of dark blue paint.

FABRICS

AS WELL as decorating the walls, ceilings, furniture and floors in your house, you can also decorate the fabrics, which themselves play a major role in any interior design scheme, particularly in the bedroom.

The choice of fabric, regardless of whether it is hand-painted, hand-printed or from a manufacturer's roll, is a key element in the overall scheme, not just in the colour and pattern it creates but also in its textural quality. Fabric comes in a wide range of thicknesses, weights and weaves, depending in part on the fibres used and the means by which they are joined to form the cloth.

From the earliest hand-woven fabrics to the big rolls that come from industrial looms, the texture is determined by the type of fibre used. Advances in technology this century have allowed us to use synthetic fibres, which have the advantage of being easy to care for, but they definitely lack the elasticity and sheer quality of natural fibres like cotton, wool, linen and silk. Nowadays, with the advent of imports from the Far East, natural fibre fabrics are no longer a more expensive option, and the range is truly breathtaking.

Whether buying ready-printed fabric or designing your own hand-painted textiles, beware of how you use pattern. Although it is perfectly possible to mix several patterns together in one room, this normally only works if there is a connecting link. In other words, you can vary the patterns, but keep the colour palette the same. Very large patterns need to be handled carefully. Not only do they involve very expensive fabric wastage in trying to match the pattern repeats, they can also dominate a small room and make it appear far smaller. In a very large room, however, they may be just what is required to bring the scale down to more normal proportions.

Different patterns have been popular at different periods. William Morris, the doyen of the Arts and Crafts movement, introduced naturalistic designs with birds, beasts and flowers. In the 1930s and 1940s, more geometric designs found favour. Country house taste has always plumped for floral or shepherdess-type designs, first made popular in the blue and white or pink and white drawn designs put on chintz by the French Toile de Jouy factory in the eighteenth century and subsequently heavily copied in England.

More recently, an eclectic mix of pattern and plain, colour and neutrals has become very popular, with simple household fabrics, like mattress ticking and calico, which are both elegant and inexpensive, becoming increasingly common. Colours preferred seem to be earthy pigments of dusty blues, rusty reds and sage greens or pale, heavily textured creams, whites and beiges.

Many companies produce co-ordinated ranges of paint, paper and fabric which certainly make the interior decorator's job much easier, but beware of overuse of mix-and-match ranges. They can induce a sense of disquiet and a strong sense of over-design if used too extensively.

Far better to take a leaf from the catalogues of some of these companies in terms of how to use these mixed-and-matched fabrics, paints and papers, and then try to work out your own rather less restrictive mix-and-match schemes, aiming to introduce a few elements that are not too obviously part of it.

However, if you want to mix different patterned fabrics, buying them from these ranges is helpful since the work is done for you in determining that the colour palette is the same, and it can be very rewarding to mix simple stripes, floral and geometric designs in a limited range of colours.

CHOICE AND CARE OF FABRICS

If you are planning to create painted designs on fabric, always do a test piece first on a small piece of the fabric you intend to use, and then launder it afterwards to check how it behaves. Calico is one of the cheapest fabrics, and being thick and evenly woven, takes most forms of paint very well.

This wonderfully creative use of pattern on both walls and bedcovers in this oriental-style bedroom is sophisticated without being cold or slick-looking. The black design on white linen and walls sets off the ornate oriental furniture. Creating disparate patterns, rather than repeating the same design, gives it a much livelier, more natural appearance, but obviously takes a great deal more work in cutting the appropriate stencils. The black and white tiled floor adds the final touch of symmetry to the colour scheme.

FABRIC TYPES

Silk There are many different kinds and grades of silk, from fine to coarse. The cheapest is what used to be known as jap or lining silk, also known as Habutai or Pongee. It is hard-wearing, smooth and shiny and is probably the best form for any novice fabric painter to practise on. It is made in various weights from very fine to reasonably heavy. You can use it for spray stencilling, sponging and saltwork.

Cotton Cotton plants are grown in different parts of the sub-tropical world, with some of the best cotton coming from Barbados (Sea Island cotton) and Egypt. It is made in various weights from very fine to really heavy canvas. Unbleached calico is cheap, solid and a very good surface for painting. It is stiff enough to make good fabric for blinds, but does not drape well. Ordinary cotton sheeting can also be used successfully, and is only a little more expensive.

Linen Made from flax, this again varies from light to heavy weight. It has an attractive sheen and an obvious weave or grain. It is not cheap, and it creases badly, but it has a very attractive quality to it, and is extremely durable.

Wool There are many different weaves and thicknesses of woollen fabric, but the ones that are best suited for painting on are fine, closely woven fabrics such as wool twill, which has a diagonal weave, and gaberdine. On softer, thicker wools, the paint may spread too much. As wool can shrink easily, be careful not to get the fabric very wet when painting on it.

Velvet This is a cut-pile fabric, made from either synthetics or from cotton. For hand-painting, cotton velvet is preferable, and some exciting effects can be achieved. Remember, however, that you cannot iron velvet direct without crushing the pile, which makes it difficult to fix those colours that require direct ironing as part of the fixing process.

Silk and linen need to be washed with care, and neither should be wrung or spun. Both must be ironed while damp. Cotton can be boiled, if necessary, and spun or wrung without problem, but only if the paint you are using can withstand it. Always check the manufacturer's instructions on textile paints and care of the fabric afterwards.

TEXTILE PAINTS

There is a growing range of textile paints for particular purposes, and you can also use ordinary household emulsion, although you cannot wash the fabric afterwards. (Lampshades or blinds, for example, could be painted with emulsion.) There are specific textile paints for use on natural and artificial fabrics, and different types have different fixing instructions. Some require baking in the oven, others fixing with a hot iron, others steam- or bath-fixing. Check the different brands and decide which one is best suited to the purpose you have in mind.

There are special textile paints for use on silk (which can also be used on cotton, wool or synthetic fibres, but the best effect is on silk, when the colour is much more luminous). There are also water-based permanent colours for use on all natural fabrics.

STENCILLING ON FABRIC

IF YOU want to stencil a pattern on to fabric, you can opt for various different media. Not all fabrics are suitable, and you will get the best results with close-woven cottons. If the fabric is very soft and absorbent, you may need to 'size' it first to prevent the paint spreading. Normally a multi-purpose PVA glue, thinned in the proportion of 40 parts PVA to 60 parts water can be used for this purpose.

Spray paints, emulsion paints and acrylic paints can all be successfully used on fabric, but if you want to be able to launder the fabric afterwards, you will have to use a proprietary product like Colourfun by Dylon.

When stencilling on fabric, make sure it is evenly stretched on a surface that will not absorb the paint. Alternatively, put plastic beneath it if necessary.

Lampshades are easy subjects for stencilling because they are already stretched, but you may find that if you use water-based paints, it pays to size the fabric first with PVA so that the paint 'bleeds' less. Stencilling on a conical shade can be slightly tricky, because you will have to organize the 'fit' of the pattern, marking it out in advance to ensure that it meets up successfully. Alternatively, create a random design, as in the one below, where this factor is not a problem.

1 You can apply the stencil pattern to the lampshade using a roller and emulsion paint (or proprietary emulsion and PVA mixture) or stencil paint with a stencil brush. Make sure the paint is sufficiently thick not to run under the stencil bridges.

2 Move the stencil along the lampshade wherever you want the pattern to appear. You can use a light spray glue to hold the stencil in place or you can use masking tape, whichever you find more convenient.

Stencilling can be carried out on many different surfaces. Here a small floor rug has been stencilled with a ribbon border pattern, echoing the colours in the stencilled border on the floor itself, and the paintwork for the windows and doors.

3 Make sure all the appropriate areas are covered. In this case, parts of the stencil pattern have been painted in wherever spaces occur, in random fashion, along the base of the shade, using only part of the stencil.

4 The finished shade. You can give it a coat of matt, polyurethane varnish if you want to be able to wipe it clean later. If you feel like it, try a reverse form of stencilling in which you stick the leaf patterns on to the shade, paint over the entire shade (leaves included) and then remove the leaves – an exact reverse of what you see here, with the background dark and the leaves pale. The light, when switched on, will shine through them.

PAINTING ON FABRIC

LTHOUGH IT is much easier to go out and buy a roll of printed fabric, the effects when you paint your own fabrics are worth the energy and effort expended. It is also far cheaper. You can buy cheap white cotton at about a third of the price of most printed fabric, and when you have painted it yourself, at least you own something which is unique. You can get very tired of seeing the same fabric designs cropping up in everyone's houses, and those that become very popular begin to look dated in a few years' time.

You do not have to be particularly skilled as a designer to paint your own fabrics, but you do need to be aware of your own limitations, both as a designer and a fabric painter. Stick to simple patterns that are easy to execute, and do not be too ambitious until you have had a little practice. Lampshades and cushion covers make good starter projects, and borders on curtains, blinds and bedlinen are also relatively easy to produce.

The range of fabrics you can paint on is large, but natural fabrics – cottons and silks in particular

These exquisite hand-painted fabrics show what can be done with imagination and flair, using different fabric painting techniques. The curtains on the left have been painted with a wax-resist pattern. Silk-screening, stencilling and block printing are other options. The blue-on-white shell pattern would be easy to copy.

– produce the best results. If you have a shop in your neighbourhood that supplies fabrics for saris, for example, you will probably find that they also have a good range of comparatively inexpensive Indian cottons and silks in plain colours, both vibrant and neutral.

One of the best areas for experimentation is in children's bedrooms. For a start, they are not particularly fussy and provided you pick designs and colours that they like, they probably will not notice any slight clumsiness on your part. They also like to ring the changes as they grow up, so you are not stuck for life with the rather ill-formed row of ducks you painted across the bottom of the roller blind! There are fabric paint kits that children can use as well, so why not involve them in the design and execution if they enjoy painting? A cushion, toy bag or nightdress case would be a good starter project for them to get involved in, or maybe a design on the corner of an old plain pillowcase. The results may be a little startling!

SALT PAINTING

This technique is used principally on silk, using purpose-designed silk textile paints, although fine cotton will produce a similar but less pronounced effect. Launder the fabric first to remove any special finishes.

The most suitable designs are either broad stripes or checks, or a completely random, abstract effect. Applying coarse sea salt to the wet painted surface causes the colours to run and change in a variety of fascinating patterns, and softly blending colours.

Salt painting is an ideal technique for cushion covers or lampshades, although you would have to make up the lampshade from the fabric after treating it as described in the steps, as you need to work on a flat, horizontal surface.

The fabric has to stretched on a frame that lifts it off the work surface, so that the paint and salt can soak in and move about freely.

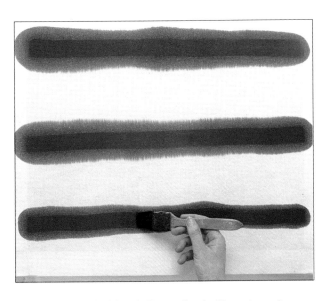

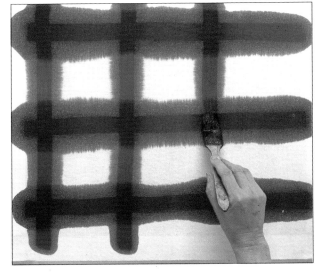

1 Stretch the fabric (ordinary calico, in this case) on a frame, using masking tape, to ensure that it is lifted off the surface so that the paint does not soak through the fabric and make it stick to the surface below. Using a small flat brush and proprietary silk paints, start to apply the first colour fairly thinly. It will spread out quite considerably.

2 Make stripes at right angles using a contrasting colour. If you paint while the first colour is still wet, the colours will bleed into each other. A more pronounced, defined line can be obtained if you wait until the first colour dries.

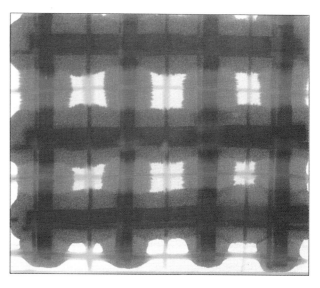

3 Create a tartan effect with thin stripes of contrasting colour, using a fine artists' brush across the centre of the squares you have painted.

4 Complete the tartan effect, by taking fine lines of the same colour through the centre of the squares as well to make the final pattern. If you want the pattern to stay fairly clearly marked, stop here.

5 While the paint is still wet, sprinkle lines of cooking salt along the outlines of the checks. This has the effect of making the colours bleed and run a great deal more than normal, creating a soft, blurred effect so very little of the white cotton is visible.

6 The finished effect in which the salt has encouraged the colours to run into each other. When the paint is dry, brush off any remaining salt and remove the fabric from the frame.

TECHNICAL INFORMATION

THE AMOUNT of paint you need for a particular paint effect depends on factors such as the absorbency of the surface and the weather on the day. The most important factor is how much you dilute the paint. Therefore, the following quantities serve only as a guide. They represent the amount of wall or wood that can be covered by undiluted paint.

Paint type	Coverage from 1 litre 2 pints	Special properties	Preparation
Water-based emulsion paint	14 sq m./ 16 sq yd	A hard-wearing finish that covers all walls easily. Quick drying and inexpensive, it comes in different finishes such as matt, silk and vinyl. The silk emulsion is washable. Difficult to wash dirt off this painted surface	Diluted with water, and coloured with universal stainers, powders, gouache and acrylics.
Polyurethane gloss	14–15 sq m/ 16–18 sq yd	A tough durable finish that is easy to apply. Wide range of colours. Needs a primer and undercoat or a previously keyed surface. Takes up to 12 hours to dry and the fumes are unpleasant.	Diluted with turpentine or white spirit, and coloured with universal stainers, artist's oil paints.
Liquid gloss	17 sq m/ 20 sq yd	A more traditional gloss finish. Needs more care to avoid drips. Requires primer and undercoat. Washes well and is durable provided the surface is well prepared and the number of coats are applied.	Diluted with turpentine and white spirit. Coloured with universal stainers and artist's oil paints.
Oil-based eggshell paint	16 sq m/ 19 sq yd	Hardwearing and good base coat for paint effects and gloss painting. It is the ideal paint for areas of high condensation such as kitchens and bathrooms.	Diluted with methylated spirit and turpentine. Coloured with universal stainers and artist's oil paints. Diluted it makes a durable colour wash (see page 76).
Primer	12 sq m/ 14 sq yd	Tough foundation coat (see page 57)	Not applicable
Artist's oil paints	—	Oil paint colours that mix with any oil-based medium to colour it. Slow drying making them ideal for paint effects. Dilute with turpentine and white spirit.	These are successful paints for colouring oil-based paints. A couple of these paints and you can create most subtle colours for ageing and antiquing. Can also be used to colour scumble glaze, varnish, oil-based paint, in fact any oil-based medium.
PVA	—	A cheap and available adhesive that can be mixed to any consistency and used as a base for mixing with colour to make your own paint.	Mix it with water and then colour with emulsion, stainers, oil colours, powder colour to make semi-gloss paint that is not waterproof.
Powder colours	—	Ground pigment that can be used to colour almost any medium to make your own paint. Dilute with water. Can mix different powders together to get different colours before diluting or colouring other bases.	Use a a tint or colour to change the colour or proprietary paints or as a tint for scumble glaze and varnishes.

BIBLIOGRAPHY

Kevin McCloud's Decorating Book
Kevin McCloud
(Dorling Kindersley, 1990).
Brilliant source of inspiration for the whole
gamut of decorating techniques. Strong on colour
combinations. Not for the novice.

Traditional Paints and Finishes
Annie Sloan and Kate Gwynn
(Collins & Brown, 1993).
Excellent background material for all the traditio-
nal paint finishes.

Art of Stencilling
Lyn Le Grice
(Viking, 1986).
Best source of inspiration on all kinds of
stencilling. Particularly good at making
stencilling look appropriate for the situation.

Hand Painted Textiles for the Home
Kazz Ball and Valerie Janitch
(David & Charles, 1991).
Useful sourcebook of a variety of fabric painting
techniques.

Decorative Découpage
Joanna Jones
(Merehurst, 1993).
Lots of découpage projects.

Paint Magic
Jocasta Innes
(Frances Lincoln, revised edition, 1992).
The book that started the fashion...

Recipes for Surfaces –
Decorative Paint Finishes Made Simple
Mandy Drucker and Pierre Finkelstein
(Cassell, 1993).
Very clear explanations of every possible kind of
paint finish.

Paintworks
Althaea Wilson
(Century, 1990).
Very painterly approach to paint finishes. Not for
the novice.

Textile Classics
Melanie Paine
(Mitchell Beazley, 1992).
Useful and inspirational reference book on types
of fabric and ideas for colour combinations.

The Complete Book of
Decorative Paint Techniques
Annie Sloan and Kate Gwynn
(Collins & Brown, 1987).
Comprehensive coverage of all forms of paint
effect.

Simple Painted Furniture
Annie Sloan and Kate Gwynn
(Dorling Kindersley, 1989).
Project-based book on furniture effects.

SUPPLIERS

IT IS worth knowing that most of the big paint manufacturers such as Leyland, Crown or Dulux have a customer services department which will help you with queries on materials for different paint finishes, so if in doubt, do consult them. J. H. Radcliffe have been specializing in high quality paints for many years, and will also answer queries. Their tins of glazes, for example, come with an extremely helpful leaflet.

L. Cornelissen & Son Ltd
105 Great Russell Street
London WC1B 3LA
Tel: 071–636 1045
Artists' materials. Pigments.
Brushes. Glazes. Fabric painting
materials.

Foxwell and James
57 Farringdon Road
London EC1M 3JH
Tel: 071–405 0152
Stockists of specialized restoring
materials, including gilding
products.

Papers and Paints
4 Park Walk
London SW10 0AD
Tel: 071–352 8626
Range of specialist paints, plus
glazes, varnishes, brushes and
pigments.

Whistler Brushes
(Lewis Ward & Co)
128 Fortune Green Road
London NW6 1DN
Tel: 071–794 3130

J. W. Bollom & Co Ltd
13 Theobalds Road
London WC1X 8FN
Tel: 071–242 0313

E. Ploton (Sundries) Ltd
273 Archway Road
London N6 5AA
Tel: 081–348 0315
All decorating materials for
glazing, stencilling and gilding.

Craig and Rose plc
172 Leith Walk
Edinburgh EH6 5EB
Tel: 031–554 1131

J. H. Radcliffe & Co
135a Linaker Street
Southport PR8 5DF
Tel: 0704 37999
Brushes, tools and glazes.

Relics
Bridge Street
Witney OX8 6DA
Tel: 0993 704611
All specialist paints, glazes,
brushes and restoration materials
as well as courses in decorative
painting.

Simpsons Paints Ltd
122–4 Broadley Street
London NW8 8BB
Tel: 071–723 6657
Specialists in gold leaf, brushes
and glazes.

Paint Magic
116 Sheen Road
Richmond
Surrey
TW9 1UR
Tel: 081–940 5503

Polyvine Ltd
Vine House
Rockhampton
Berkeley
Glos GL13 9DT
Tel: 0454 261276
Suppliers of acrylic paint
products.

Index

ACKNOWLEDGEMENTS

I would like to thank Annie Sloan for creating the techniques shown in this book, and for reading the manuscript. The courses she runs at Relics in Witney (see page 126) are a wonderful introduction to paint effects. I would also like to thank Geoff Dann for the step-by-step photography and Alison Leach and Richard Carr for their respective editorial and design input.

Picture Acknowledgements

Cassell
pages 11, 23, 108 David George; pages 28–29, 62, 80 Geoff Dann

Step-by-step photography Geoff Dann

Elizabeth Whiting Associates
pages 2–3, 8, 10, 14, 19, 20, 24, 26, 31, 34, 39, 40, 45, 48, 50, 55, 56, 59, 60, 66, 69, 74, 77, 88, 91, 93, 94, 104, 106, 113, 120

Marianne Majerus
pages 18, 47, 96, 107

Robert Harding Picture Library
page 12 Simon Brown/*Country Homes and Interiors*; pages 16–17 Brian Harrison; page 36 *Country Homes and Interiors*; pages 84, 87, 117, 121 JHC Wilson